W9-BKW-950

THE GREAT ENIGMA

NEW COLLECTED POEMS

AIR MAIL (färdig?)

på jakt efter en brevlåda
bar jag brevet genom stan.
I storskogen av sten och betong
fladdrade denna vilsna fjäril.

Frimärkets flygande matta.
Adressens berusade bokstäver.
plus min förseglade sanning
som flyger just nu över havet.

Atlantens krypande silver.
Molnbankarna. Fiskebåten
som en utspottad olivkärna.
Och kölvattnets bleka ärr.

Mitt arbete ~~rör sig~~ rör sig sakta.
Jag sneglar inte på klockan.
Träskskuggorna är svarta siffror
i den girigs tystnaden.

Och sanningen finns på marken
där ingen vågar ta den.
Sanningen ligger på gatan.
Ingen gör den till sin.

Tomas Tranströmer

The Great Enigma
New Collected Poems

Translated from the Swedish by Robin Fulton

 A NEW DIRECTIONS BOOK

NEW HANOVER COUNTY
PUBLIC LIBRARY
201 CHESTNUT STREET
WILMINGTON, NC 28401

Copyright © 1987, 1997, 2002, 2006 by Tomas Tranströmer

Translation copyright © 1987, 1997, 2002, 2006 by Robin Fulton

All rights reserved. Except for brief passages quoted in a newspaper, magazine, radio, or television review, no part of this book may be reproduced in any form or by any means, electronic or mechanical, including photocopying and recording, or by any information storage and retrieval system, without permission in writing from the Publisher.

The Great Enigma: New Collected Poems is published by arrangement with Bloodaxe Books Ltd., Highgreen, Tarset, Northumberland, NE48 1RP, UK.

Manufactured in the United States of America.
New Directions Books are printed on acid-free paper.
First published as a New Directions Paperbook (NDP1050) in 2006.
Published simultaneously in Canada by Penguin Books Canada Limited.

Library of Congress Cataloging-in-Publication Data

Tranströmer, Tomas, 1931-
[Poems. English. Selections]
The great enigma : new collected poems / Tomas Tranströmer ; translated from the Swedish by Robin Fulton.
p. cm.
Includes index.
ISBN-13: 978-0-8112-1672-2 (alk. paper)
ISBN-10: 0-8112-1672-1 (alk. paper)
1. Tranströmer, Tomas, 1931—Translations into English. I. Fulton, Robin. II. Title.
PT9876.3.R3A2 2006
839.71'74--dc22

10 9 8 7 6

New Directions Books are published for James Laughlin
by New Directions Publishing Corporation
80 Eighth Avenue, New York, NY 10011
www.ndpublishing.com

Contents

PRISON (*FÄNGELSE*), 1959

THE HALF-FINISHED HEAVEN (*DEN HALVFÄRDIGA HIMLEN*), 1962

BELLS AND TRACKS (*KLANGER OCH SPÅR*), 1966

SEEING IN THE DARK (MÖRKERSEENDE), 1970

PATHS (STIGAR), 1973

BALTICS (ÖSTERSJÖAR), 1974

FOR THE LIVING AND THE DEAD (FÖR LEVANDE OCH DÖDA), 1989

THE SAD GONDOLA (SORGEGONDOLEN), 1996

THE GREAT ENIGMA (DEN STORA GÅTAN), 2004

PROSE MEMOIR
MEMORIES LOOK AT ME (*MINNENA SER MIG*), 1993

Foreword

Over forty years ago Tomas Tranströmer wrote a poem called "Morning Birds," which concludes with the idea of the poem growing while the poet shrinks:

> It grows, it takes my place.
> It pushes me aside.
> It throws me out of the nest.
> The poem is ready.

He could hardly have envisaged then how aptly these lines would describe his career. On the one hand we have the private person who was born in Stockholm in 1931, who spent many years in Västerås working as a psychologist, and who has now returned to Stockholm to live in the very area in which he grew up. The same private person has spent as much time as possible out in the Stockholm Archipelago, on Runmarö, an island rich in family associations and a place which, I suspect, he feels is his real home. As part of the private person's story it has to be recorded that just short of his sixtieth birthday he suffered a stroke which deprived him of most of his speech and partly inhibited movement on his right side.

On the other hand we have the poet whose gathered work takes up very little space on the bookshelf—as he says in the memoir of his grammar-school days, he became "well-known for deficient productivity"—and yet this poet's seemingly modest body of work has generated enormous interest. For over half a century, as they slowly accumulated, his poems have attracted special attention in his native Sweden, and in the course of the last three decades they have caught the interest of an extraordinary range of readers throughout the world. The ever-widening response to Tranströmer's poems has been meticulously documented by Lennart Karlström: the first two volumes of his bibliography, taking us up to 1999, amount to almost eight hundred pages and list translations into fifty languages.

Tranströmer is perhaps less in need of selection or pruning than any other poet. A new reader, however, might not want to proceed through this volume in a straight chronological manner. Reading back from recent to early work could be more helpful than reading forward (as in the arrangement of May Swenson's selection *Windows and Stones*, University of Pittsburgh Press, 1972). But whichever direction the new reader wants to take, a few pointers may help.

17 Poems (1954) gathered pieces written by Tranströmer in his late teens and very early twenties and immediately announced the presence of a distinct poetic personality. The three longer pieces that conclude the collection suggest a kind of poetic ambition which the young Tranströmer soon lost—his notes on my first version of "Elegy," for instance, contain remarks like: "This poem was written by a romantic 22-year-old!" and "Oh dear, how complicated I was in my younger days. . . ." But the very first poem, suitably called "Prelude," reveals a quality characteristic of all his writing: the very sharply realized visual sense of his poems. The images leap out from the page, so the first-time reader or listener has the immediate feeling of being given something very tangible. "Prelude" also points forward thematically. It describes the process of waking up (note how this process appears not in the usual terms of rising to the surface but in terms of falling, of a parachute jump down into a vivid and teeming world). And this fascination with the borders between sleep and waking, with the strange areas of access between an everyday world we seem to know and another world we can't know in the same way but whose presence is undeniable—such a fascination has over the decades been one of Tranströmer's predominant themes. "Dream Seminar," for example, from *The Wild Market Square* (1983) deals directly with certain aspects of the relations between waking and dreaming states, but the reader will soon discover many poems which explore this region.

The way in which Tranströmer describes, or allows for, or tries to come to terms with the powerful elements of our lives that we cannot consciously control or even satisfactorily define suggests, rightly, that there is a profoundly religious aspect to his poems. In a largely secular country like Sweden such a writer may well be asked about religion in a rather blunt or naive manner (as if "Do you believe in God?" were the same kind of question as "Do you vote Social Democrat?") and Tranströmer has always replied to such questions cautiously. The following, from an interview with Gunnar Harding in 1973, is a characteristic response to the comment that reviewers sometimes refer to him as a mystic and sometimes as a religious poet:

> Very pretentious words, mystic and so on. Naturally I feel reserved
> about their use, but you could at least say that I respond to reality in

such a way that I look on existence as a great mystery and that at times, at certain moments, this mystery carries a strong charge, so that it does have a religious character, and it is often in such a context that I write. So these poems are all the time pointing toward a greater context, one that is incomprehensible to our normal everyday reason. Although it begins in something very concrete.

This movement toward a larger context is very important, and it reflects Tranströmer's distrust of oversimplified formulations, slogans, and rhetorical gestures as shortcuts that can obscure and mislead. It is in similar terms that we can see his response (or perhaps refusal to respond directly) to the criticism of several reviewers of the late 1960s and early 1970s that his poetry ignored current political "realities." The assumption behind such criticism was that poetry is just another element of political debate, and its use of language is no different from an editorial. Many of his poems do deal with current "realities," but with a careful avoidance of the simplifications and aggressions of politicized language and with an awareness of a wider and deeper context that seemed beyond the range of the directly "engaged" poetry of the period, with its concern for taking "positions" on a black-and-white and rather parochial political map. See in particular "About History" from *Bells and Tracks* (1966), and then "By the River," "Outskirts," "Traffic," and "Night Duty" from *Seeing in the Dark* (1970).

To return to the religious aspect—the reader will notice how specifically or overtly religious allusions in the early poetry soon disappear from succeeding work. This has been interpreted as a process of secularization: I would rather see it as a way of trying to do without the shorthand of everyday religious terminology in order to try to define for oneself those areas in which a sense of immanence may be experienced. We see something of this attempt in poems like "Secrets on the Way" and "Tracks," both in Tranströmer's 1958 collection *Secrets on the Way,* where a series of contrasts, or similes, or just luminously clear images, are grouped as if around a central space where some kind of epiphany is happening. Such poems end by returning us, perhaps abruptly, to an active world, but they leave us with the feeling that a strangeness has crossed our path.

Later forms of this development seem to entail two processes. First, we can see some attempt to be more specific about this central space or crossing-point, about this intrusion that can illuminate or disturb our normal way of life: here we can find paradoxes, imagery from and about dreams, speculations about how both past and future can impinge upon the present, investigations into memory, and a fascination with the many ways in which borders, open and closed, may be experienced. Second, we find a gradual move away from the impersonality of the early poetry. Tranströmer can still use the third-person singular as a means of giving distance to what is clearly first-person singular experience—but from the late 1960s and the early 1970s we can watch an increasingly open involvement of Tranströmer's own personality as an element in the poems. This is partly a matter of allowing more of the concrete starting point of the poem to appear (Tranströmer can name a birthplace for nearly all of his poems), but it is also, more importantly, a matter of letting himself appear in his poems as, in a sense, an actor in his own dramas, both acting and being acted upon or through. This process can be clearly followed in poems such as: "Lament," in *The Half-Finished Heaven* (1962); "Crests," "Winter's Formulae," and "Alone" in *Bells and Tracks* (1966); "Preludes," "Upright," and "The Bookcase" in *Seeing in the Dark* (1970); and "The Outpost" and "December Evening 1972" in *Paths* (1973).

The lines of development I have roughly indicated reach a peak—or perhaps a wave crest may be more appropriate, for it is something in motion—in *Baltics* (1974), Tranströmer's longest poem to date and one that marked a new expansiveness in his manner. Note the plural of the title: here we have not one Baltic but a whole series of them, reflecting the very different experience of those in whose lives that particular sea has come to play a part—some of these Baltics overlap, while some apparently contradict each other. The poem seems to have been under way by about 1970, and two external stimuli helped as starting points. One was the finding of a logbook kept by Tranströmer's maternal grandfather in the 1880s, listing the ships he piloted. The other was his reading of Edward Lucie-Smith's English translation of part of Jean Paul de Dadelsen's *Jonah*, which suggested to him a manner or tone of voice for a long poem less monumental than the accents of Eliot in *Four Quartets*. A third element should be mentioned, and that is Tranströmer's lifelong interest in poems whose growth parallels musical development: for instance, the three long pieces that conclude *17 Poems* (and which were originally meant to constitute one long poem) were intended to represent a parallel to passacaglia form, and "The Four Temperaments" in *Secrets on the Way* aimed to echo Hindemith's Theme and Variations: "The Four Temperaments" for piano and string orchestra. Reference to specific musical works plays an impor-

tant part in poems like "Schubertiana" in *The Truthbarrier* (1978) and the ti-
tle poem of *The Sad Gondola* (1996). Tranströmer himself has claimed that
the writing of *Baltics* was his "most consistent attempt to write music." Be-
sides its pattern of thematic return and variation that recalls similar pat-
terns in many musical works, Tranströmer has further remarked that it is
in part a polemic against his earlier self, against the way in which his ear-
lier poems from the Stockholm archipelago treated the area as a pro-
tected oasis or reserve, whereas *Baltics* treats the landscape and its life as
open to the threats of the surrounding world.

The more relaxed manner of *Baltics* does not imply a more casual struc-
ture, however. It is not difficult for the reader new to the work to notice
the archlike patterning of themes, as outlined by the Danish critic Steen
Andersen:

> Part Six, about the grandmother . . . is a parallel to Part One, about the
> grandfather; in both cases there is documentary knowledge about the
> family (photo, logbook) and in both cases the poet himself must in-
> quire his way forward as regards other details of this past. From Part
> One, the sea, we are taken, in Part Two, to the land, but with many ref-
> erences to the life which Part One introduced and described to us; the
> churchyard stones seen by the I-figure unite past and present. In Part
> Three the I-figure is more present still, but here, too, mainly through
> observations of things left by the past (the font, a photo). Parts Four
> and Five describe immediate observations, as distinct from the family
> and historical memories we otherwise find in the book. And finally
> Part Six carries us back to the past (the grandmother) and to the pres-
> ent, especially in the closing lines. . . . It is thus a matter of *people* in a
> particular *place.*

In its amplification of this outline, Kjell Espmark's account of *Baltics* lets
us see the sequence as a climax in Tranströmer's work up to the early
1970s, and Espmark argues that we must look to its themes to get to the
heart of the poem. On the one hand we have distances, obstacles or fron-
tiers; on the other we have attempts to overcome these, and even in-
stances of spontaneous contact:

> The distance or blockage can change from one section to another—
> from historical and geographical distance to emotional isolation and

the inability to articulate what "wants to be said." The, bridging-over theme is modulated accordingly. The tension between the limiting and the uniting movements condenses in one point—a genuinely Tranströmerian oxymoron—"the open frontier." It is toward this epiphanously charged point that the movements of the poem strive.

Baltics was not followed by anything quite so extended, but the freer use of long lines can be seen in several poems in subsequent volumes. Ideally, such poems ought to be printed on broad pages so that the long lines can be seen to be long, not broken off and carried over. These volumes contain also a dozen or so prose poems, but what is more interesting is the presence (especially in the 1980s) of an increasing number of very short and sometimes cryptic pieces. The brevity of the poems written in the 1990s may well be related to the effects of the poet's illness, but it does seem that a tendency toward such compression was already in evidence before 1990.

In order to illustrate some of the foregoing, and also to give some idea of the poet's own approach to his poems, it may be interesting to give a few examples of Tranströmer's own comments:

The Journey's Formulae (*Secrets on the Way*)
Here is a man plowing. It means something. Why have I now for half a year seen this man plowing? No, it'll soon be a whole year. What does it mean? A month ago I finally understood what would happen. It's in Yugoslavia. At first I thought it was in a Swedish landscape in autumn—I was tricked by the lighting. No, it's Yugoslavia, in the middle of the day, and the sun is burning. It has something to do with the war. Or at least there are many dead people in the background—they move away later but what is really going on? It's no epic, it's a bagatelle, five lines perhaps. Yet terribly important to me . . . [Letter to Göran Palm, 1956]

In the Nile Delta (*The Half-Finished Heaven*)
In the first place it is a direct description of something I actually experienced. It is not something I invented—I recount in the concentrated form of the poem the experiences of a day in the town of Tanta in Egypt in 1959. I and my wife (who was only nineteen then and had never before been confronted with the reality of a poor country) had with difficulty managed to escape from the tour guides—there was never any help available

if it was a matter of making one's way into parts of the country which the authorities did not want to show foreigners—and there we were in Tanta. It could be asked why I use "he" instead of "I" in the poem—I think it is a way of giving distance and generality to a difficult and troubling experience. I have tried to write as unsentimentally and nakedly as possible and mainly with monosyllabic words. Well—we went to sleep in the indescribably dirty ex-hotel and then I dreamt what is in the poem. The words which a "voice" said were somewhat different—as often happens in dreams the words were nonsense words, but they had the meaning I've given them in the poem. The dream helped me, it created a change of mood from negative feelings and hate toward something else—not to a "reconciliation" with the suffering around us but toward a way of seeing such suffering without running away. If I were to philosophize about this, I would say that I believe hate and rage are a first and natural reaction to the plight of poor countries but they don't give much inspiration to do anything about the situation. In the dream there was a strong positive element, a sort of GOOD WILL. My immediate reaction to this experience was of a religious nature and a trace of this can be seen, for instance, in the third-to-last line, in the words alluding to the Gospel account of the sick people around the pool in Bethesda—when the water was stirred, the pool received its miracle-working power (John 5:2). [In reply to a question from Mats Dahlberg, 1968]

Night Duty (*Seeing in the Dark*)
That bell-ringing at the end of "Night Duty"—when I was walking around in the old Västerås churchyard, which was in the process of being dug up, and caught sight of the digging machine's scoop, bell-ringing broke out from the Lutheran cathedral tower and it seemed to wrap the whole experience in something that each reader can interpret as he pleases, but which for me is in part something fatefully apocalyptic but also something like the sponge of religious faith reaching down from above to swab one's face as one sits like a beaten boxer in the corner of the ring waiting for the next round (the last one?). [Letter to Göran Palm, 1970]

The Outpost (*Paths*)
It began almost as a joke. It began very modestly. There was no intention it should become such a serious business; it was more something I passed

the time with. This is the situation: I'm on a military exercise and get posted out to a heap of stones, a situation one experiences as quite absurd. And to cheer myself up a little I wrote the opening lines. I didn't mean for any poem to come out of it. These first verses were written very easily just because I didn't have any feeling of "now this is serious, you must achieve something." But then gradually the poem came to deal with how I find myself in an absurd situation in life generally, as I often do. Life puts us in certain absurd situations and it's impossible to escape. And that's where the poem becomes very serious, in the fifth verse, which ends: "I am the place / where creation is working itself out." This kind of religious idea recurs here and there in my poems of late, that I see a kind of meaning in being present, in using reality, in experiencing it, in making something of it. And I have an inkling that I'm doing this as some sort of task or commission. It recurs further on in the book at the beginning of "December Evening 1972":

> Here I come, the invisible man, perhaps employed
> by a Great Memory to live right now. . . .

It's a purely personal experience really, that I fulfill some function here, in the service of something else. This sounds pretentious and so the tone in such circumstances often becomes a little frivolous. [Conversation with Gunnar Harding, 1973]

Citoyens (*The Truthbarrier*)

In 1970, I had an old Saab that had just been tested for roadworthiness. The verdict was that everything was in splendid order, including the brakes. Then, when I was on the highway, I found myself in a lane where everyone was driving fairly fast. Suddenly the cars in front of me slowed down. I stepped on the brakes but nothing happened. I drove straight into the back of a Mercedes. My poor little car was like an accordion. I survived. I stepped out. All I walked away with was a shirt, a pair of trousers, shoes, and a book about the French Revolution. It was quite a shaking experience. I had a dream that night, which is what I have recounted in the poem: I have not invented anything. Except perhaps the image of "the plummet/ that makes the clocks go . . ." [Conversation with Robert Bly, 1977]

The Gallery (*The Truthbarrier*)
"The Gallery" is the poem I've carried around longest. It began some ten years ago with a particular experience. I was in Laxå as a teacher on a course for social workers, teaching interview techniques. One evening I went to the motel to sleep and then had a sort of Judgment Day experience: what is it I'm really doing? I'm a psychologist, after all, so I ought to be an expert in interviewing people. Playing one's professional role comes easily, and in that role one is to a high degree protected. But now it was as if I was confronted with what my job really meant. It was a very disturbing evening. I lay there and watched the images of a whole crowd of people I had met in my job unwind like a film, and suddenly I seemed to experience them as a human being, not just as a professional. The poem is quite simply a coming-to-terms with this professional role, even if I started writing it as a rhapsody on authentic life stories. Yes, all those fates glimpsed in the poem are authentic, and I myself am there too, in the passage beginning "An artist said . . ." There you find a self-portrait, which was actually written in quite another context but which I inserted here. I thought that I, too, belonged in the gallery. [Conversation with Matts Rying, 1979]

Female Portrait, 19th Century (*For the Living and the Dead*)
I amused myself making a rhythmically exact version, perhaps in very bad English. It turned out like this:

> Strangled by the clothing, her voice. Her eyes are
> on the gladiator. Then she herself is
> out in the arena. And free? A gilt frame
>   bear hugs the picture.

Proper sapphic meter! But we don't have to be so pedantic. We could forget about the sapphics and write something like this:

> Her voice is choked in the dress. While her eyes
> follow the gladiator. Then it is she who
> stands on the arena. How free? A gilt frame
>   strangles the painting.

". . . it is she who / stands on the arena"—to me it's important to get in this idea "she herself" somehow. After all, she does in a way change places with the gladiator. If you write only "Then she's out in the arena," the only way of emphasizing *she* is to italicize the word, and that looks silly. Another problem is "bear hugs." "Björnkram" in Swedish sounds quite pleasant and suggests a strong and jovial fellow heartily embracing someone.... "Gastkramar" is of course not at all hearty. It is almost the worst expression of anguish that Swedes have. We'll have to discuss this. What a dreadful amount of talk about this little poem. But it's the poem I myself like best in the whole book. Hence the hypochondria. [Letter to Robin Fulton; July 8, 1989]

•

I have been trying to make English versions of Tranströmer's poems for at least thirty-five years. The many translations published in a wide variety of magazines are enumerated in Karlström's bibliography. Every now and then a gathering was published in book form. First came a selection from Penguin Books in 1974. A larger one was published by Ardis Books (Ann Arbor) in 1981. The first collected edition was brought out by Bloodaxe Books in 1987, and ten years later replaced by the *New Collected Poems*, from the same publisher. The latter contained, as additions to the previous book, two recent collections of poems, from 1989 and 1996, as well as the autobiographical chapters "Memories Look at Me."

All the poems Tomas Tranströmer has published in book form are contained in this revised and expanded New Directions edition. This includes Tranströmer's 2004 volume *The Great Enigma*—a group of five small poems followed by forty-five even smaller haiku—as well as a group of nine other haiku, *Prison*, written in 1959 and previously uncollected. Whether a Japanese haiku master would feel on common ground with the mentality behind these Swedish examples of the form, I have no idea. I prefer to regard them simply as a set of syllabic poems (whose syllabic count I have matched) with an ability to surprise and puzzle that far exceeds what we might expect from their miniature dimensions. I would particularly like to record my thanks to Tomas Tranströmer for his unfailing help over the years.

Robin Fulton [2006]

THE GREAT ENIGMA
NEW COLLECTED POEMS

17 POEMS

17 DIKTER

1954

• I •

Prelude

Waking up is a parachute jump from dreams.
Free of the suffocating turbulence the traveler
sinks toward the green zone of morning.
Things flare up. From the viewpoint of the quivering lark
he is aware of the huge root systems of the trees,
their swaying underground lamps. But aboveground
there's greenery—a tropical flood of it—with
lifted arms, listening
to the beat of an invisible pump. And he
sinks toward summer, is lowered
in its dazzling crater, down
through shafts of green damp ages
trembling under the sun's turbine. Then it's checked,
this straight-down journey through the moment, and the wings spread
to the osprey's repose above rushing waters.
The Bronze Age trumpet's
outlawed note
hovers above the bottomless depths.

In day's first hours consciousness can grasp the world
as the hand grips a sun-warmed stone.
The traveler is standing under the tree. After
the crash through death's turbulence, shall
a great light unfold above his head?

· II ·

AUTUMNAL ARCHIPELAGO

Storm

Here the walker suddenly meets the giant
oak tree, like a petrified elk whose crown is
furlongs wide before the September ocean's
           murky green fortress.

Northern storm. The season when rowanberry
clusters swell. Awake in the darkness, listen:
constellations stamping inside their stalls, high
           over the treetops.

Evening—Morning

Moon—its mast is rotten, its sail is shriveled.
Seagull—drunk and soaring away on currents.
Jetty—charred rectangular mass. The thickets
           founder in darkness.

Out on doorstep. Morning is beating, beats on
ocean's granite gateways and sun is sparkling
near the world. Half-smothered, the gods of summer
           fumble in sea mist.

Ostinato

Under the buzzard's circling point of stillness
ocean rolls resoundingly on in daylight,
blindly chews its bridle of weed and snorts up
       foam over beaches.

Earth is veiled in darkness where bats can sense their
way. The buzzard stops and becomes a star now.
Ocean rolls resoundingly on and snorts up
       foam over beaches.

· III ·

Five Stanzas to Thoreau

Yet one more abandoned the heavy city's
ring of greedy stones. And the water, salt and
crystal, closes over the heads of all who
        truly seek refuge.

     ·

Silence slowly spiraling up has risen
here from earth's recesses to put down roots and
grow and with its burgeoning crown to shade his
        sun-heated doorstep.

     ·

Kicks a mushroom thoughtlessly. Thunderclouds are
piling on the skyline. Like copper trumpets
crooked roots of trees are resounding, foliage
        scatters in terror.

     ·

Autumn's headlong flight is his weightless mantle,
flapping till again from the frost and ashes
peaceful days have come in their flocks and bathe their
        claws in the wellspring.

     ·

Disbelief will meet him who saw a geyser
and escaped from wells filled with stones, like Thoreau
disappearing deep in his inner greenness
        artful and hopeful.

Gogol

The jacket threadbare as a wolf pack.
The face like a marble slab.
Sitting in the circle of his letters in the grove that rustles
with scorn and error,
the heart blowing like a scrap of paper through the inhospitable
passageways.

The sunset is now creeping like a fox over this country,
igniting the grass in a mere moment.
Space is full of horns and hooves and underneath
the barouche glides like a shadow between my father's
lit courtyards.

St. Petersburg on the same latitude as annihilation
(did you see the beauty in the leaning tower)
and around the ice-bound tenements floating like a jellyfish
the poor man in his cloak.

And here, enveloped in fasts, is the man who before was surrounded by
        the herds of laughter,
but these have long since taken themselves to tracts far above the tree line.
Men's unsteady tables.
Look outside, see how darkness burns hard a whole galaxy of souls.
Rise up then on your chariot of fire and leave the country!

Sailor's Yarn

There are bare winter days when the sea is kin
to mountain country, crouching in grey plumage,
a brief minute blue, long hours with waves like pale
lynxes vainly seeking hold in the beach gravel.

On such a day wrecks might come from the sea searching
for their owners, settling in the town's din, and drowned
crews blow landward, thinner than pipe smoke.

(The real lynxes are in the north, with sharpened claws
and dreaming eyes. In the north, where day
lives in a mine both day and night.

Where the sole survivor may sit
at the borealis stove and listen
to the music of those frozen to death.)

Strophe and Counter-Strophe

The outermost circle belongs to myth. There the helmsman sinks upright
among glittering fish-backs.
How far from us! When day
stands in a sultry windless unrest—
as the Congo's green shadow holds
the blue men in its vapor—
when all this driftwood on the heart's sluggish
coiling current
piles up.

Sudden change: in under the repose of the constellations
the tethered ones glide.
Stern high, in a hopeless
position, the hull of a dream, black
against the coastline's pink. Abandoned
the year's plunge, quick
and soundless—as the sledge-shadow, doglike, big—
travels over snow,
reaches the wood.

Agitated Meditation

A storm drives the mill sails wildly round
in the night's darkness, grinding nothing. —You
   are kept awake by the same laws.
The grey shark belly is your weak lamp.

Shapeless memories sink to the sea's depths
and harden there to strange columns. —Green
   with algae is your crutch. A man
who takes to the seas comes back stiffened.

The Stones

The stones we threw I hear
fall, glass-clear through the years. In the valley
the confused actions of the moment
fly screeching from
treetop to treetop, become silent
in thinner air than the present's, glide
like swallows from hilltop
to hilltop until they've
reached the furthest plateaus
along the frontier of being. There all
our deeds fall
glass-clear
with nowhere to fall to
except ourselves.

Context

Look at the grey tree. The sky has run
through its fibers down in the earth—
only a shrunk cloud is left when
the earth has drunk. Stolen space
is twisted in pleats, twined
to greenery. —The brief moments
of freedom rise in us, whirl
through the Parcae and further.

Morning Approach

The black-backed gull, the sun-captain, holds his course.
Beneath him is the water.
The world is still sleeping like a
multicolored stone in the water.
Undeciphered day. Days—
like Aztec hieroglyphs.

The music. And I stand trapped
in its Gobelin weave with
raised arms—like a figure
out of folk art.

There Is Peace in the Surging Prow

On a winter morning you feel how this earth
plunges ahead. Against the house walls
an air current smacks
out of hiding.

Surrounded by movement: the tent of calm.
And the secret helm in the migrating flock.
Out of the winter gloom
a tremolo rises

from hidden instruments. It is like standing
under summer's high lime tree with the din
of ten thousand
insect wings above your head.

Midnight Turning Point

The wood ant watches silently, looks into
nothing. And nothing's heard but drips from dim
leafage and the night's murmuring deep in
    summer's canyon.

The spruce stands like the hand of a clock,
spiked. The ant glows in the hill's shadow.
Bird cry! And at last. The cloud-packs slowly
    begin to roll.

· IV ·

Song

The gathering of white birds grew: gulls
dressed in canvas from the sails of foundered ships
but stained by vapors from forbidden shores.

Alarm! Alarm! around refuse from a cargo boat.
They crowded in and formed an ensign-staff
that signaled "Booty here."

And gulls careered across watery wastes
with blue acres gliding in the foam.
Athwart, a phosphorescent pathway to the sun.

But Väinämöinen travels in his past
on oceans glittering in ancient light.
He rides. The horse's hooves are never wet.

Behind: the forest of his songs is green.
The oak whose leap's a thousand years long.
The mighty windmill turned by birdsong.

And every tree a prisoner in its soughing.
With giant cones glinting in the moonlight
when the distant pine glows like a beacon.

Then the Other rises with his spell
and the arrow, seeing far and wide, flees,
the feather singing like a flight of birds.

A dead second when the horse abruptly
stiffens, breaks across the waterline
like a blue cloud beneath the thunder's antenna.

And Väinämöinen plunges heavy in the sea
(a jumping-sheet the compass points hold tight).
Alarm! Alarm! among the gulls around his fall!

Like one bewitched, without anxiety,
standing at the center of the picture
of his joy, eleven corn sheaves bulging.

Reliance—an alp-top humming in the ether
three thousand meters up where the clouds sail
races. The puffed basking shark wallows

guffawing soundlessly beneath the sea.
(Death and renewal when the wave arrives.)
And peacefully the breezes cycle through the leaves.

On the horizon thunder rumbles dully
(as the herd of buffalo flees in its dust).
The shadow of a fist clenches in the tree

and strikes down him who stands bewitched
in his joyous picture where the evening sky
seems to glow behind the wild boar's mask of clouds.

His double, envious, arranges
a secret rendezvous with his woman.
And the shadow gathers and becomes a tidal wave

a tidal wave with riding sea gulls darkened.
And the port-side heart sizzles in a breaker.
Death and renewal when the wave arrives.

The gathering of white birds grew: gulls
dressed in canvas from the sails of foundered ships
but stained by vapors from forbidden shores.

The herring gull: a harpoon with a velvet back.
In closeup like a snowed-in hull
with hidden pulses glittering in rhythm.

His flier's nerves in balance. He soars.
Footless hanging in the wind he dreams
his hunter's dream with his beak's sharp shot.

He plunges to the surface, full-blossomed greed,
crams and jerks himself around his booty
as if he were a stocking. And then he rises like a spirit.

(Energies—their context is renewal,
more enigmatic than the eel's migrations.
A tree, invisible, in bloom. And as

the grey seal in its underwater sleep
rises to the surface, takes a breath,
and dives—still asleep—to the seabed

so now the Sleeper in me secretly
has joined with *that* and has returned while I
stood staring fixedly at something else.)

And the diesel engine's throbbing in the flock
past the dark skerry, a cleft of birds
where hunger blossomed with stretched maw.

At nightfall they could still be heard:
an abortive music like that from
the orchestra pit before the play begins.

But on his ancient sea Väinämöinen drifted
shaken in the squall's mitt or supine
in the mirror-world of calms where the birds

were magnified. And from a stray seed, far
from land at the sea's edge growing
out of waves, out of a fogbank it sprang:

a mighty tree with scaly trunk, and leaves
quite transparent and behind them
the filled white sails of distant suns

glided on in trance. And now the eagle rises.

· V ·

Elegy

At the outset. Like a fallen dragon
in some mist- and vapor-shrouded swamp,
our spruce-clad coastland lies. Far out there:
two steamers crying from a dream

in the fog. This is the lower world.
Motionless woods, motionless surface
and the orchid's hand that reaches from the soil.
On the other side, beyond these straits

but hanging in the same reflection: the Ship,
like the cloud hanging weightless in its space.
And the water around its prow is motionless,
becalmed. And yet—a storm is up!

and the steamer smoke blows level—the sun
flickers there in its grip—and the gale
is hard against the face of him who boards.
To make one's way up the port side of Death.

A sudden draft, the curtain flutters.
Silence ringing, an alarm clock.
A sudden draft, the curtain flutters.
Until a distant door is heard closing

far off in another year.

•

O field as grey as the buried bog-man's cloak.
And island floating darkly in the fog.
It's quiet, as when the radar turns
and turns its arc in hopelessness.

There's a crossroads in a moment.
Music of the distances converges.
All grown together in a leafy tree.
Vanished cities glitter in its branches.

From everywhere and nowhere a song
like crickets in the August dark. Embedded
like a wood beetle, he sleeps here in the night,
the peat bog's murdered traveler. The sap compels

his thoughts up to the stars. And deep
in the mountain: here's the cave of bats.
Here hang the years, the deeds, densely.
Here they sleep with folded wings.

One day they'll flutter out. A throng!
(From a distance, smoke from the cave mouth.)
But still their summer-winter sleep prevails.
A murmuring of distant waters. In the dark tree

a leaf that turns.

•

One summer morning a harrow catches
in dead bones and rags of clothing. —He
lay there after the peat bog was drained
and now stands up and goes his way in light.

In every parish eddies golden seed
around ancient guilt. The armored skull
in the plowed field. A wanderer en route
and the mountain keeps an eye on him.

In every parish the marksman's rifle hums
at midnight when the wings unfold
and the past expands in its collapse
and darker than the heart's meteorite.

An absence of spirit makes the writing greedy.
A flag begins to smack. The wings
unfold around the spoils. This proud journey!
where the albatross ages to a cloud

in Time's jaws. And culture is a whaling
station where the stranger walks
among white gables, playing children, and
still with each breath he takes he feels

the murdered giant's presence.

•

Soft black-cock crooning from the heavenly spheres.
The music, guiltless in our shadow, like
the fountain water rising among the wild beasts,
deftly petrified around the playing jets.

The bows disguised, a forest.
The bows like rigging in a torrent—
the cabin's smashed beneath the torrent's hooves—
within us, balanced like a gyroscope, is joy.

This evening the world's calm is reflected
when the bows rest on strings without being moved.
Motionless in mist the forest trees
and the water-tundra mirroring itself.

Music's voiceless half is here, like the scent
of resin rising from lightning-damaged spruce.
An underground summer for each of us.
There at the crossroads a shadow breaks free

and runs off to where the Bach trumpet points.
Sudden confidence, by grace. To leave behind
one's self-disguise here on this shore
where the wave breaks and slides away, breaks

and slides away.

Epilogue

December. Sweden is a beached
unrigged ship. Against the twilight sky
its masts are sharp. And twilight lasts
longer than day—the road here is stony:
not till midday does the light arrive
and winter's coliseum rise
lit by unreal clouds. At once
the white smoke rises, coiling from
the villages. The clouds are high on high.
The sea snuffles at the tree-of-heaven's roots
distracted, as if listening to something else.
(Over the dark side of the soul
there flies a bird, wakening
the sleepers with its cries. The refractor
turns, catches in another time,
and it is summer: mountains bellow, bulged
with light and the stream raises the sun's glitter
in transparent hand . . . All then gone
as when a film spills out of a projector.)

Now the evening star burns through the cloud.
Houses, trees, and fences are enlarged, grow
in the soundless avalanche of darkness.
And beneath the star more and more develops
of the other, hidden landscape, that which lives
the life of contours on the night's x-ray.
A shadow pulls its sledge between the houses.
They are waiting.
                    Six o'clock—the wind
gallops thunderously along the village street,
in darkness, like a troop of horsemen. How
the black turmoil resounds and echoes!
The houses trapped in a dance of immobility,
the din like that of dreams. Gust upon gust
staggers over the bay away

to the open sea that tosses in the dark.
In space the stars signal desperately.
They're lit and quenched by headlong clouds
that only when they shade the light betray
their presence, like clouds of the past that scud
through souls. When I walk past
the stable wall I hear in all that noise
the sick horse tramping inside.
And there's departure in the storm,
by a broken gate that bangs and bangs, a lamp
swaying from a hand, a beast that cackles
frightened on the hill. Departure in the thunderous
rumble over the byre roofs, the roaring
in the telephone wires, the shrill whistling
in the tiles on night's roof
and the tree tossing helplessly.

A wail of bagpipes is let loose! A wail
of bagpipes keeping step! Liberators.
A procession. A forest on the march!
A bow wave seethes and darkness stirs,
and land and water move. And the dead,
hidden under deck, they are with us,
with us on the way: a voyage, a journey
which is no wild rush but gives security.
And the world is always taking down its tent
anew. One summer day the wind takes hold
of the oak's rigging, hurls Earth forward.
The lily paddles with its hidden webbed foot
in the pond's embrace—the pond which is in flight.
A boulder rolls away in the halls of space.
In the summer twilight islands seem to rise
on the horizon. Old villages are on
their way, retreating further into woods
on the seasons' wheels with magpie creaking.
When the year kicks off its boots, and the sun
climbs higher, the trees break out in leaves
and take the wind and sail out in freedom.

Below the mountain breaks the pinewood surf,
but summer's long warm groundswell comes,
flows through the treetops slowly, rests
a moment, sinks away again—
a leafless coast remains. And finally:
God's spirit, like the Nile: flooding
and sinking in a rhythm calculated
in texts from many epochs.

But He is also the immutable
and thus observed here seldom. It's from
the side He crosses the procession's path.

As when the steamer passes through the mist,
the mist that does not notice. Silence.
Faint glimmer of the lantern is the signal.

SECRETS ON THE WAY

HEMLIGHETER PÅ VÄGEN

1958

· I ·

Solitary Swedish Houses

A confusion of black spruce
and smoking moonbeams.
Here's the cottage lying low
and not a sign of life.

Till the morning dew murmurs
and an old man opens
—with a shaky hand—his window
and lets out an owl.

Further off, the new building
stands steaming
with the laundry butterfly
fluttering at the corner

in the middle of a dying wood
where the moldering reads
through spectacles of sap
the proceedings of the bark-drillers.

Summer with flaxen-haired rain
or one solitary thundercloud
above a barking dog.
The seed is kicking inside the earth.

Agitated voices, faces
fly in the telephone wires
on stunted rapid wings
across the moorland miles.

The house on an island in the river
brooding on its stony foundations.
Perpetual smoke—they're burning
the forest's secret papers.

The rain wheels in the sky.
The light coils in the river.
Houses on the slope supervise
the waterfall's white oxen.

Autumn with a gang of starlings
holding dawn in check.
The people move stiffly
in the lamplight's theater.

Let them feel without alarm
the camouflaged wings
and God's energy
coiled up in the dark.

The Man Who Awoke with Singing over the Roofs

Morning. May rain. The city is still quiet
as a mountain hamlet. The streets quiet. And in
the sky a bluish-green aero-engine rumbles. —
        The window is open.

The dream where the sleeper is lying prostrate
turns transparent. He stirs, begins
groping for attention's instruments—
        almost in space.

Weather Picture

The October sea glistens coldly
with its dorsal fin of mirages.

Nothing is left that remembers
the white dizziness of yacht races.

An amber glow over the village.
And all sounds in slow flight.

A dog's barking is a hieroglyph
painted in the air above the garden

where the yellow fruit outwits
the tree and drops of its own accord.

The Four Temperaments

The probing eye turns the sun's rays into police batons.
And in the evening: the hubbub from a party in the room below
sprouts up through the floor like unreal flowers.

Driving on the plain. Darkness. The coach seemed stuck on the spot.
An anti-bird screeched in starry emptiness.
The albino sun stood over tossing dark seas.

•

A man like an uprooted tree with croaking foliage
and lightning at attention saw the beast-smelling
sun rise up among pattering wings on the world's

rocky island surging ahead behind banners of foam through night
and day with white sea birds howling
on the deck and all with a ticket to Chaos.

•

You need only close your eyes to hear plainly
the gulls' faint Sunday over the sea's endless parish.
A guitar begins twanging in the thicket and the cloud dawdles

slowly as the green sledge of late spring
—with the whinnying light in the shafts—
comes gliding on the ice.

•

Woke with my girl's heels clopping in the dream
and outside two snowdrifts like winter's abandoned gloves
while leaflets from the sun cascaded over the city.

The road never comes to an end. The horizon rushes ahead.
The birds shake in the tree. The dust whirls around the wheels.
All the rolling wheels that contradict death!

Caprichos

It's getting dark in Huelva: sooty palm trees
and the train whistle's flurrying
silver-white bats.

The streets have been filled up with people.
And the woman hurrying in the throng cautiously weighs
the last daylight on the balance of her eyes.

The office windows are open. You can still hear
how the horse is tramping inside.
The old horse with the rubber-stamp hooves.

Not till midnight are the streets empty.
At last in all the offices: it's blue.

Up there in space:
trotting silently, sparkling and black,
unseen and unbound,
having thrown its rider:
a new constellation I call "The Horse."

· II ·

Siesta

The stones' Whitsun. And with sparkling tongues . . .
The city without weight in the midday hours.
Burials in simmering light. The drum which drowns
locked-in eternity's pounding fists.

The eagle rises and rises over the sleepers.
Sleep where the mill wheel turns like thunder.
Tramping from the horse with blindfolded eyes.
Locked-in eternity's pounding fists.

The sleepers hang like weights in the tyrants' clock.
The eagle drifts dead in the sun's streaming white current.
And echoing in time—as in Lazarus's coffin—
locked-in eternity's pounding fists.

Izmir at Three O' Clock

Just ahead in the almost empty street
two beggars, one without legs—
he's carried on the other one's back.

They stood—as on a midnight road an animal
stands blinded staring into the headlights—
for one moment before passing on

and scuttled across the street like boys
in a playground while the midday heat's
myriad of clocks ticked in space.

Blue flowed past on the waters, flickering.
Black crept and shrank, stared from stone.
White blew up to a storm in the eyes.

When three o'clock was tramped under hooves
and darkness pounded in the wall of light
the city lay crawling at the sea's door

gleaming in the vulture's telescopic sight.

· III ·

Secrets on the Way

Daylight struck the face of a man who slept.
His dream was more vivid
but he did not wake.

Darkness struck the face of a man who walked
among the others in the sun's strong
impatient rays.

It was suddenly dark, like a downpour.
I stood in a room that contained every moment—
a butterfly museum.

And the sun still as strong as before.
Its impatient brushes were painting the world.

Tracks

2 AM: moonlight. The train has stopped
out in the middle of the plain. Far away, points of light in a town,
flickering coldly at the horizon.

As when someone has fallen into a dream so deep
he'll never remember having been there
when he comes back to his room.

As when someone has fallen into an illness so deep
everything his days were becomes a few flickering points, a swarm,
cold and tiny on the horizon.

The train is standing quite still.
2 AM: bright moonlight, few stars.

Kyrie

Sometimes my life opened its eyes in the dark.
A feeling as if crowds drew through the streets
in blindness and anxiety on the way toward a miracle,
while I invisibly remain standing.

As the child falls asleep in terror
listening to the heart's heavy tread.
Slowly, slowly until morning puts its rays in the locks
and the doors of darkness open.

· IV ·

A Man from Benin

*(On a photograph of a fifteenth-century relief in bronze
from the African state of Benin, showing a Portuguese Jew.)*

When darkness fell I was still
but my shadow pounded
against the drumskin of hopelessness.
When the pounding began to ease
I saw the image of an image
of a man coming forward
in the emptiness, a page
lying open.
Like going past a house
long since abandoned
and someone appears at the window.
A stranger. He was the navigator.
He seemed to take notice.
Came nearer without a step.
In a hat that shaped itself
imitating our hemisphere
with the brim at the equator.
The hair parted in two fins.
The beard hung curled
around his mouth like eloquence.
He held his right arm bent.
It was thin like a child's.
The falcon that should have had its place
on his arm grew out
from his features.
He was the ambassador.
Interrupted in the middle of a speech
which the silence continues
even more forcibly.
Three peoples were silent in him.

He was the image of three peoples.
A Jew from Portugal,
who sailed away with the others,
the drifting and the waiting ones,
the hunched-up flock
in the caravel that was
their rocking wooden mother.
Landfall in a strange air
which made the atmosphere furry.
Observed in the marketplace
by the African castmaker.
Long in his eyes' quarantine.
Reborn in the race of metal:
"I am come to meet him
who raises his lantern
to see himself in me."

Balakirev's Dream
(1905)

The black grand piano, the gleaming spider
trembled at the center of its net of music.

In the concert hall a land was conjured up
where stones were no heavier than dew.

But Balakirev dozed off during the music
and dreamed a dream about the czar's droshky.

It rumbled over the cobblestones
straight into the crow-cawing blackness.

He sat alone inside the cab and looked
and also ran alongside on the road.

He knew the journey had lasted long
and his watch showed years, not hours.

There was a field where the plow lay
and the plow was a fallen bird.

There was an inlet where the vessel lay
icebound, lights out, with people on deck.

The droshky glided there across the ice
and the wheels spun with a sound of silk.

A lesser battleship: *Sebastopol.*
He was aboard. The crew gathered around.

"You won't die if you can play."
They showed him a curious instrument.

Like a tuba, or a phonograph,
or a part of some unknown machine.

Stiff with fear and helpless he knew: it is
the instrument that drives the man-of-war.

He turned toward the nearest sailor,
made signs despairingly, and begged:

"Cross yourself, like me, cross yourself!"
The sailor stared sadly like a blind man,

stretched out his arms, sank his head—
he hung as if nailed in the air.

The drums beat. The drums beat. Applause!
Balakirev woke from his dream.

The wings of applause pattered in the hall.
He saw the man at the grand piano rise.

Outside the streets lay darkened by the strike.
The droshkies were rushing through the dark.

· V ·

After an Attack

The sick boy.
Locked in a vision
with his tongue stiff as a horn.

He sits with his back turned to the picture of the cornfield.
The bandage around his jaw hinting at embalming.
His glasses are thick like a diver's. And everything is unanswered
and vehement like the telephone ringing in the dark.

But the picture behind him—a landscape that gives peace though the
        grain is a golden storm.
Sky like blueweed and drifting clouds. Beneath in the yellow surge
some white shirts are sailing: reapers—they cast no shadows.

There's a man standing far across the field and he seems to be looking this
        way.
A broad hat darkens his face.
He seems to be observing the dark figure here in the room, perhaps to
        help.
Imperceptibly the picture has begun widening and opening behind the
        sick brooding
invalid. It sparks and pounds. Every grain is ablaze to rouse him!
The other—in the corn—gives a sign.

He has come close.
No one notices.

• VI •

The Journey's Formulae

(from the Balkans, 1955)

1

A murmur of voices behind the plowman.
He doesn't look around. The empty fields.
A murmur of voices behind the plowman.
One by one the shadows break loose
and plunge into the summer sky's abyss.

2

Four oxen come, under the sky.
Nothing proud about them. And the dust thick
as wool. The insects' pens scrape.

A swirl of horses, lean as in
grey allegories of the plague.
Nothing gentle about them. And the sun raves.

3

The stable-smelling village with thin dogs.
The party official in the market square
in the stable-smelling village with white houses.

His heaven accompanies him: it is high
and narrow like inside a minaret.
The wing-trailing village on the hillside.

4

An old house has shot itself in the forehead.
Two boys kick a ball in the twilight.
A swarm of rapid echoes. —Suddenly, starlight.

5

On the road in the long darkness. My wristwatch
gleams obstinately with time's imprisoned insect.

The quiet in the crowded compartment is dense.
In the darkness the meadows stream past.

But the writer is halfway into his image, there
he travels, at the same time eagle and mole.

PRISON

FÄNGELSE

1959

NINE HAIKU FROM HÄLLBY YOUNG OFFENDERS' PRISON

Prison

Eleven-a-side
sudden dismay—the ball's gone
right over the wall.

•

More noise than need be
just to startle time into
getting a move on.

•

Wrongly spelled, those lives—
loveliness remains, the way
tattoo-marks remain.

•

When the runaway
was caught he'd gathered pockets-
ful of chanterelles.

•

Din from the workshops
and the watchtower's heavy steps
perplexed the forest.

•

The tall doors swing back.
We're inside the prison yard
in a new season.

•

The wall lamps are lit—
the night-flier sees a smudge
of unreal brightness.

•

An enormous truck
rumbles past at night. The dreams
of inmates tremble.

•

The boy drinks milk and
sleeps securely in his cell,
a mother of stone.

THE HALF-FINISHED HEAVEN

DEN HALVFÄRDIGA HIMLEN

1962

· I ·

The Couple

They switch off the light and its white shade
glimmers for a moment before dissolving
like a tablet in a glass of darkness. Then up.
The hotel walls rise into the black sky.

The movements of love have settled, and they sleep
but their most secret thoughts meet as when
two colors meet and flow into each other
on the wet paper of a schoolboy's painting.

It is dark and silent. But the town has pulled closer
tonight. With quenched windows. The houses have approached.
They stand close up in a throng, waiting,
a crowd whose faces have no expressions.

The Tree and the Sky

There's a tree walking around in the rain,
it rushes past us in the pouring grey.
It has an errand. It gathers life
out of the rain like a blackbird in an orchard.

When the rain stops so does the tree.
There it is, quiet on clear nights
waiting as we do for the moment
when the snowflakes blossom in space.

Face to Face

In February living stood still.
The birds flew unwillingly and the soul
chafed against the landscape as a boat
chafes against the pier it lies moored to.

The trees stood with their backs turned to me.
The deep snow was measured with dead straws.
The footprints grew old out on the crust.
Under a tarpaulin language pined.

One day something came to the window.
Work was dropped, I looked up.
The colors flared. Everything turned around.
The earth and I sprang toward each other.

Ringing

And the thrush blew its song on the bones of the dead.
We stood under a tree and felt time sinking and sinking.
The churchyard and the schoolyard met and widened into each other
       like two streams in the sea.

The ringing of the church bells rose to the four winds borne by the gentle
       leverage of gliders.
It left behind a mightier silence on earth
and a tree's calm steps, a tree's calm steps.

Through the Wood

A place called Jacob's Marsh
is the summer day's cellar
where the light sours to a drink
tasting of old age and slums.

The feeble giants stand entangled
closely—so nothing can fall.
The cracked birch molders there
in an upright position like a dogma.

From the bottom of the wood I rise.
It grows light between the trunks.
It is raining over my roofs.
I am a waterspout for impressions.

At the edge of the wood the air is warm.
Great spruce, turned away and dark
whose muzzle hidden in the earth's mold
drinks the shadow of a shower.

November with Nuances of Noble Fur

It is the sky's being so grey
that makes the ground begin to shine:
the meadows with their timid green,
the plowed fields dark as black bread.

There is the red wall of a barn.
And the acres under water
like shining rice paddies in an Asia—
the gulls stand there reminiscing.

Misty spaces deep in the woods
chiming softly against each other.
Inspiration that lives secluded
and flees among the trees like Nils Dacke.

• II •

The Journey

In the underground station.
A crowding among placards
in a staring dead light.

The train arrived and collected
faces and portfolios.

Darkness next. We sat
in the carriages like statues,
hauled through the caverns.
Restraint, dreams, restraint.

In stations under sea level
they sold the news of the dark.
People in motion sadly
silently under the clock dials.

The train carried
outer garments and souls.

Glances in all directions
on the journey through the mountain.
Still no change.

But nearer the surface a murmuring
of bees began—freedom.
We stepped out of the earth.

The land beat its wings
once and became still
under us, widespread and green.

Ears of corn blew in
over the platforms.

Terminus—I
followed on, further.

How many were with me? Four,
five, hardly more.

Houses, roads, skies,
blue inlets, mountains
opened their windows.

C Major

When he came down to the street after the rendezvous
the air was swirling with snow.
Winter had come
while they lay together.
The night shone white.
He walked quickly with joy.
The whole town was downhill.
The smiles passing by—
everyone was smiling behind turned-up collars.
It was free!
And all the question marks began singing of God's being.
So he thought.

A music broke out
and walked in the swirling snow
with long steps.
Everything on the way toward the note C.
A trembling compass directed at C.
One hour higher than the torments.
It was easy!
Behind turned-up collars everyone was smiling.

Noon Thaw

The morning air delivered its letters with stamps that glowed.
The snow shone and all burdens lightened—a kilo weighed just 700
      grams.

The sun was high over the ice hovering on the spot both warm and cold.
The wind came out gently as if it were pushing a pram.

Families came out, they saw open sky for the first time in ages.
We found ourselves in the first chapter of a very gripping story.

The sunshine stuck to all the fur caps like pollen on bees
and the sunshine stuck to the name WINTER and stayed there till winter
      was over.

A still life of logs on the snow made me thoughtful. I asked them:
"Are you coming along to my childhood?" They answered "Yes."

In among the copses there was a murmuring of words in a new language:
the vowels were blue sky and the consonants were black twigs and the
      speech was soft over the snow.

But the jet plane curtsying in its skirts of noise
made the silence on earth even stronger.

When We Saw the Islands Again

As the boat draws near
a sudden downpour blinds it.
Quicksilver shot bounces on the water.
The blue-grey lies down.

The sea's in the cottages too.
A stream of light in the dark hallway.
Heavy steps upstairs
and chests with newly ironed smiles.
An Indian orchestra of copper pans.
A baby with eyes all at sea.

(The rain starts disappearing.
The smoke takes a few faltering steps
in the air above the roofs.)

Here comes more
bigger than dreams.

The beach with the hovels of elms.
A notice with the word CABLE.
The old heathery moor shines
for someone who comes flying.

Behind the rocks rich furrows
and the scarecrow our outpost
beckoning the colors to itself.

An always-bright surprise
when the island reaches out a hand
and pulls me up from sadness.

From the Hilltop

I stand on the hill and look across the bay.
The boats rest on the surface of summer.
"We are sleepwalkers. Moons adrift."
So say the white sails.

"We slip through a sleeping house.
We gently open the doors.
We lean toward freedom."
So say the white sails.

Once I saw the wills of the world sailing.
They held the same course—one single fleet.
"We are dispersed now. No one's escort."
So say the white sails.

• III •

Espresso

The black coffee they serve outdoors
among tables and chairs gaudy as insects.

Precious distillations
filled with the same strength as Yes and No.

It's carried out from the gloomy kitchen
and looks into the sun without blinking.

In the daylight a dot of beneficent black
that quickly flows into a pale customer.

It's like the drops of black profoundness
sometimes gathered up by the soul,

giving a salutary push: Go!
Inspiration to open your eyes.

· IV ·

The Palace

We stepped in. A single vast hall,
silent and empty, where the surface of the floor lay
like an abandoned skating rink.
All doors shut. The air grey.

Paintings on the walls. We saw
pictures throng lifelessly: shields, scale-
pans, fishes, struggling figures
in a deaf-and-dumb world on the other side.

A sculpture was set out in the void:
in the middle of the hall alone a horse stood
but at first when we were absorbed
by all the emptiness we did not notice him.

Fainter than the breathing in a shell
sounds and voices from the town
circling in this desolate space
murmuring and seeking power.

Also something else. Something darkly
set itself at our senses' five
thresholds without stepping over them.
Sand ran in every silent glass.

It was time to move. We walked
over to the horse. He was gigantic,
dark as iron. An image of power itself
abandoned when the princes left.

The horse spoke: "I am The Only One.
The emptiness that rode me I have thrown.
This is my stable. I am growing quietly.
And I eat the silence that's in here."

Syros

In Syros harbor leftover cargo steamers lay waiting.
Prow by prow by prow. Moored many years since:
CAPE RION, Monrovia.
KRITOS, Andros.
SCOTIA, Panama.

Dark pictures on the water, they have been hung away.

Like toys from our childhood that have grown to giants
and accuse us
of what we never became.

XELATROS, Pireus.
CASSIOPEIA, Monrovia.
The sea has read them through.

But the first time we came to Syros, it was at night,
we saw prow by prow by prow in the moonlight and thought:
What a mighty fleet, magnificent connections.

In the Nile Delta

The young wife wept over her food
in the hotel after a day in the city
where she saw the sick creep and huddle
and children bound to die of want.

She and her husband went to their room.
Sprinkled water to settle the dirt.
Lay on their separate beds with few words.
She fell in a deep sleep. He lay awake.

Out in the darkness a great noise ran past.
Murmurs, tramping, cries, carts, songs.
All in want. Never came to a stop.
And he sank in sleep curled in a No.

A dream came. He was on a voyage.
In the grey water a movement swirled
and a voice said: "There is one who is good.
There is one who can see all without hating."

· V ·

A Dark Swimming Figure

About a prehistoric painting
on a rock in the Sahara:
a dark swimming figure
in an old river which is young.

Without weapons or strategy,
neither at rest nor quick,
and cut from his own shadow
gliding on the bed of the stream.

He struggled to make himself free
from a slumbering green picture,
to come at last to the shore
and be one with his own shadow.

Lament

He laid aside his pen.
It rests still on the table.
It rests still in the empty room.
He laid aside his pen.

Too much that can neither be written nor kept silent!
He is paralyzed by something happening far away
although the wonderful traveling bag throbs like a heart.

Outside it is early summer.
Whistlings from the greenery—men or birds?
And cherry trees in bloom embrace the trucks that have come home.

Weeks go by.
Night comes slowly.
The moths settle on the windowpane:
small pale telegrams from the world.

Allegro

I play Haydn after a black day
and feel a simple warmth in my hands.

The keys are willing. Soft hammers strike.
The resonance green, lively, and calm.

The music says freedom exists
and someone doesn't pay the emperor tax.

I push down my hands in my Haydnpockets
and imitate a person looking on the world calmly.

I hoist the Haydnflag—it signifies:
"We don't give in. But want peace."

The music is a glasshouse on the slope
where the stones fly, the stones roll.

And the stones roll right through
but each pane stays whole.

The Half-Finished Heaven

Despondency breaks off its course.
Anguish breaks off its course.
The vulture breaks off its flight.

The eager light streams out,
even the ghosts take a draft.

And our paintings see daylight,
our red beasts of the Ice Age studios.

Everything begins to look around.
We walk in the sun in hundreds.

Each man is a half-open door
leading to a room for everyone.

The endless ground under us.

The water is shining among the trees.

The lake is a window into the earth.

Nocturne

I drive through a village at night, the houses rise up
in the glare of my headlights—they're awake, want to drink.
Houses, barns, signs, abandoned vehicles—now
they clothe themselves in Life. —The people are sleeping:

some can sleep peacefully, others have drawn features
as if training hard for eternity.
They don't dare let go though their sleep is heavy.
They rest like lowered crossing barriers when the mystery draws past.

Outside the village the road stretches far among the forest trees.
And the trees the trees keeping silence in concord with each other.
They have a theatrical color, like firelight.
How distinct each leaf! They follow me home.

I lie down to sleep, I see strange pictures
and signs scribbling themselves behind my eyelids
on the wall of the dark. Into the slit between wakefulness and dream
a large letter tries to push itself in vain.

A Winter Night

The storm puts its mouth to the house
　　and blows to produce a note.
I sleep uneasily, turn, with shut eyes
　　read the storm's text.

But the child's eyes are large in the dark
　　and for the child the storm howls.
Both are fond of lamps that swing.
　　Both are halfway toward speech.

The storm has childish hands and wings.
　　The Caravan bolts toward Lapland.
And the house feels its own constellation of nails
　　holding the walls together.

The night is calm over our floor
　　(where all expired footsteps
rest like sunk leaves in a pond)
　　but outside the night is wild.

Over the world goes a graver storm.
　　It sets its mouth to our soul
and blows to produce a note. We dread
　　the storm will blow us empty.

BELLS AND TRACKS

KLANGER OCH SPÅR

1966

Portrait with Commentary

Here is a portrait of a man I knew.
He's sitting at the table, his newspaper open.
The eyes settle down behind the glasses.
The suit is washed with the shimmer of pinewoods.

It's a pale and half-complete face. —
Yet he always inspired trust. Which is why
people would hesitate to come near him
for fear of meeting some misfortune.

His father earned money like dew.
But no one felt secure at home—
always a feeling that alien thoughts
broke into the house at night.

The newspaper, that big dirty butterfly,
the chair and the table and the face are at rest.
Life has stopped in big crystals.
But may it stop there only till further notice!

●

That which is I in him is at rest.
It exists. He doesn't notice
and therefore it lives, exists.

What am I? Now and then long ago
I came for a few seconds quite close
to ME, to ME, to ME.

But the moment I caught sight of ME
I lost ME — there was only a hole
through which I fell like Alice.

Lisbon

In the Alfama quarter the yellow tramcars sang on the steep slopes.
There were two prisons. One was for thieves.
They waved through the grilled windows.
They shouted to be photographed.

"But here," said the conductor giggling like a split man,
"here sit politicians." I saw the façade the façade the façade
and high up in a window a man
who stood with a telescope to his eye and looked out over the sea.

Laundry hung in blue air. The walls were hot.
The flies read microscopic letters.
Six years later I asked a woman from Lisbon:
"Is it true, or have I dreamt it?"

From an African Diary
(1963)

On the Congolese marketplace pictures
shapes move thin as insects, deprived of their human power.
It's a hard passage between two ways of life.
He who has arrived has a long way to go.

A young man found a foreigner lost among the huts.
Didn't know whether to take him for a friend or a subject for extortion.
His doubt disturbed him. They parted in confusion.

The Europeans mostly stay clustered by the car as if it were Mama.
The crickets are as strong as electric razors. The car drives home.
Soon the beautiful darkness comes, taking charge of the dirty clothes.
      Sleep.
He who has arrived has a long way to go.

It helps perhaps with handshakes like a flight of migratory birds.
It helps perhaps to let the truth out of the books.
It is necessary to go further.

The student reads in the night, reads and reads to be free
and having passed his exam he becomes a step for the next man.
A hard passage.
He who has gone furthest has a long way to go.

Crests

With a sigh the elevators begin to rise
in high blocks delicate as porcelain.
It will be a hot day out on the asphalt.
The traffic signs have drooping eyelids.

The land a steep slope to the sky.
Crest after crest, no proper shadow.
We hunt for You, flying
through the summer in cinemascope.

And in the evening I lie like a ship
with lights out, just at the right distance
from reality, while the crew
swarms in the parks ashore.

Hommages

Walked along the antipoetic wall.
Die Mauer. Don't look over.
It wants to surround our adult lives
in the routine city, the routine landscape.

Eluard touched some button
and the wall opened
and the garden showed itself.

I used to go with the milk pail through the wood.
Purple trunks on all sides.
An old joke hung
as beautiful as a votive ship.

Summer read out of *Pickwick Papers*.
The good life, a tranquil carriage
crowded with excited gentlemen.

Close your eyes, change horses.

In distress come childish thoughts.
We sat by the sickbed and prayed
for a pause in the terror, a breach
where the Pickwicks could pull in.

Close your eyes, change horses.

It is easy to love fragments
that have been on the way a long time.
Inscriptions on church bells
and proverbs written across saints
and many-thousand-year-old seeds.

Archilochos! —No answer.

The birds roamed over the seas' rough pelt.
We locked ourselves in with Simenon
and felt the smell of human life
where the serials debouch.

Feel the smell of truth.

The open window has stopped
in front of the treetops
and the evening sky's farewell letter.

Shiki, Björling, and Ungaretti
with life's chalks on death's blackboard.
The poem which is completely possible.

I looked up when the branches swung.
White gulls were eating black cherries.

Winter's Formulae

1

I fell asleep in my bed
and woke up under the keel.

At four o'clock in the morning
when life's clean-picked bones
coldly associate with one another.

I fell asleep among the swallows
and woke up among the eagles.

2

In the lamplight the ice on the road
is gleaming like lard.

This is not Africa.
This is not Europe.
This is nowhere other than "here."

And that which was "I"
is only a word
in the December dark's mouth.

3

The institute's pavilions
displayed in the dark
shine like TV screens.

A hidden tuning fork
in the great cold
sends out its tone.

I stand under the starry sky
and feel the world creep
in and out of my coat
as in an anthill.

4

Three dark oaks sticking out of the snow.
So gross, but nimble-fingered.
Out of their giant bottles
the greenery will bubble in spring.

5

The bus crawls through the winter evening.
It glimmers like a ship in the spruce forest
where the road is a narrow deep dead canal.

Few passengers: some old and some very young.
If it stopped and quenched the lights
the world would be deleted.

Morning Birds

I waken the car
whose windshield is coated with pollen.
I put on my sunglasses.
The birdsong darkens.

Meanwhile another man buys a paper
at the railway station
close to a large goods wagon,
which is all red with rust
and stands flickering in the sun.

No blank space anywhere here.

Straight through the spring warmth a cold corridor
where someone comes running
and tells how up at the head office
they slandered him.

Through a back door in the landscape
comes the magpie
black and white.
And the blackbird darting to and fro
till everything becomes a charcoal drawing,
except the white clothes on the washingline:
a Palestrina chorus.

No blank space anywhere here.

Fantastic to feel how my poem grows
while I myself shrink.
It grows, it takes my place.
It pushes me aside.
It throws me out of the nest.
The poem is ready.

About History

1

One day in March I go down to the sea and listen.
The ice is as blue as the sky. It is breaking up under the sun.
The sun that also whispers in a microphone under the covering of ice.
It gurgles and froths. And someone seems to be shaking a sheet far out.
It's all like History: our Now. We are submerged, we listen.

2

Conferences like flying islands about to crash . . .
Then: a long trembling bridge of compromises.
There shall the whole traffic go, under the stars,
under the unborn pale faces,
outcast in the vacant spaces, anonymous as grains of rice.

3

Goethe traveled in Africa in '26 disguised as Gide and saw everything.
Some faces become clearer from everything they see after death.
When the daily news from Algeria was read out
a large house appeared with all the windows blackened,
all except one. And there we saw the face of Dreyfus.

4

Radical and Reactionary live together as in an unhappy marriage,
molded by each other, dependent on each other.
But we who are their children must break loose.
Every problem cries in its own language.
Go like a bloodhound where the truth has trampled.

5

Out on the open ground not far from the buildings
an abandoned newspaper has lain for months, full of events.
It grows old through nights and days in rain and sun,
on the way to becoming a plant, a cabbage head, on the way to being
       united with the earth.
Just as a memory is slowly transmuted into your own self.

Alone

1

One evening in February I almost died here.
The car skidded sideways on the ice, out
onto the wrong side of the road. The approaching cars—
their lights—closed in.

My name, my girls, my job
broke free and were left silently behind
farther and farther away. I was anonymous
like a boy in a playground surrounded by enemies.

The approaching traffic had huge lights.
They shone on me while I pulled at the wheel
in a transparent terror that floated like egg white.
The seconds grew—there was space in them—
they grew as big as hospital buildings.

You could almost pause
and breathe for a while
before being crushed.

Then something caught: a helping grain of sand
or a wonderful gust of wind. The car broke free
and scuttled smartly right over the road.
A post shot up and cracked—a sharp clang—it
flew away in the darkness.

Then—stillness. I sat back still in my seatbelt
and saw someone coming through the whirling snow
to see what had become of me.

2

I have been walking for a long time
on the frozen Östergötland fields.
I have not seen a single person.

In other parts of the world
there are people who are born, live, and die
in a perpetual crowd.

To be always visible—to live
in a swarm of eyes—
a special expression must develop.
Face coated with clay.

The murmuring rises and falls
while they divide among themselves
the sky, the shadows, the sand grains.

I must be alone
ten minutes in the morning
and ten minutes in the evening.
—Without a program.

Everyone is lining up at everyone's door.

Many.

One.

On the Outskirts of Work

In the middle of work
we start longing fiercely for wild greenery,
for the Wilderness itself, penetrated only
by the thin civilization of telephone wires.

•

The moon of leisure circles the planet Work
with its mass and weight. —That's how they want it.
When we are on our way home the ground pricks up its ears.
The underground listens to us via the grassblades.

•

Even in this working day there is a private calm.
As in a smoky inland area where a canal flows:
THE BOAT appears unexpectedly in the traffic
or glides out behind the factory, a white vagabond.

•

One Sunday I walk past an unpainted new building
that stands in front of a grey wet surface.
It is half finished. The wood has the same light color
as the skin on someone bathing.

•

Outside the lamps the September night is totally dark.
When the eyes adjust, there is faint light
over the ground where large snails glide out
and the mushrooms are as numerous as the stars.

After Someone's Death

Once there was a shock
that left behind a long pale glimmering comet's tail.
It contains us. It blurs TV images.
It deposits itself as cold drops on the aerials.

You can still shuffle along on skis in the winter sun
among groves where last year's leaves still hang.
They are like pages torn from old telephone directories—
the names are eaten up by the cold.

It is still beautiful to feel your heart throbbing.
But often the shadow feels more real than the body.
The samurai looks insignificant
beside his armor of black dragon scales.

Oklahoma

1

The train stopped far south. It was snowing in New York.
Here you could go about in shirtsleeves the whole night.
But no one was out. Only the cars
flew past in their glare, flying saucers.

2

"We battlefields who are proud
of our many dead . . ."
said a voice while I wakened.

The man behind the counter said:
"I'm not trying to sell it,
I'm not trying to sell it,
I only want you to look at it."
And he showed the Indians' axes.

The boy said:
"I know I have a prejudice,
I don't want to be left with it, sir.
What do you think of us?"

3

This motel is a strange shell. With a hired car
(a huge white servant outside the door)
almost without memory and without ploy
at last I can settle on my point of balance.

Summer Plain

We have seen so much.
Reality has used us up so much,
but here is summer at last:

a large airfield—the flight controller is bringing down
load after load of frozen
people from space.

The grass and the flowers—here we land.
The grass has a green manager.
I report myself.

Downpour over the Interior

The rain is hammering on the car roofs.
The thunder rumbles. The traffic slows down.
Headlights are on in the middle of the summer day.

Smoke pours down chimneys.
All living things huddle, shut their eyes.
A movement inwards, feel life stronger.

The car is almost blind. He stops
lights a private fire and smokes
while the water swills along the windows.

Here on a forest road, winding and out of the way
near a lake with water lilies
and a long mountain that vanishes in the rain.

Up there lie piles of stones
from the Iron Age when this was a place
for tribal wars, a colder Congo

and the danger drove beasts and men together
to a murmuring refuge behind the walls,
behind thickets and stones on the hilltop.

A dark slope, someone moving
up clumsily with his shield on his back
—this he imagines while his car is standing.

It begins to lighten, he rolls down the window.
A bird flutes away to itself
in a thinning silent rain.

The lake surface is taut. The thunder-sky whispers
down through the water lilies to the mud.
The forest windows are slowly opening.

But the thunder strikes out of the stillness!
A deafening clap. And then a void
where the last drops fall.

In the silence he hears an answer coming.
From far away. A kind of coarse child's voice.
It rises, a bellowing from the hill.

A roar of mingled notes.
A long-hoarse trumpet from the Iron Age.
Perhaps from inside himself.

Under Pressure

The blue sky's engine drone is deafening.
We're living on a shuddering worksite
where the ocean depths can suddenly open up—
shells and telephones hiss.

You can see beauty only from the side, hastily.
The dense grain on the field, many colors in a yellow stream.
The restless shadows in my head are drawn there.
They want to creep into the grain and turn to gold.

Darkness falls. At midnight I go to bed.
The smaller boat sets out from the larger boat.
You are alone on the water.
Society's dark hull drifts farther and farther away.

Open and Closed Spaces

A man feels the world with his work like a glove.
He rests for a while at midday having laid aside the gloves on the shelf.
They suddenly grow, spread,
and black out the whole house from inside.

The blacked-out house is away among the winds of spring.
"Amnesty," runs the whisper in the grass: "amnesty."
A boy sprints with an invisible line slanting up in the sky
where his wild dream of the future flies like a kite bigger than the suburb.

Further north you can see from a summit the endless blue carpet of pine
          forest
where the cloud shadows
are standing still.
No, are flying.

An Artist in the North

I, Edvard Grieg, moved like a free man among men.
Ready with a joke, read the papers, traveled here and there.
Led the orchestra.
The concert hall with its lamps trembling in triumph like the train-ferry
        when it puts in.

I have brought myself up here to be shut in with silence.
My work-cottage is small.
The piano a tight fit like the swallow under the eaves.

For the most part the beautiful steep slopes say nothing.
There is no passageway
but sometimes a little hatch opens
and lets out a strangely seeping light direct from trolldom.

Reduce!

And the hammer blows in the mountain came
came
came
came one spring night into our room
disguised as a beating of the heart.

The year before I die I'll send out four hymns to track down God.
But it starts here.
A song about what is near.

What is near.

The battlefield within us
where we, the Bones of the Dead,
fight to become living.

In the Open

1

Late autumn labyrinth.
At the entrance to the wood a discarded empty bottle.
Go in. At this season the woods are silently deserted halls.
Only a few kinds of noise: as if someone were cautiously removing twigs
        with tweezers
or a hinge creaking faintly inside a thick tree trunk.
The frost has breathed on the mushrooms and they have shriveled.
They are like objects and garments found after a disappearance.
Now twilight comes. It's a matter of getting out
and seeing your landmarks again: the rusty implement in the field
and the house on the other side of the lake, a russet square strong as a
        bouillon cube.

2

A letter from America set me off, drove me out
one light night in June on the empty streets in the suburb
among newborn blocks without memory, cool as blueprints.

The letter in my pocket. Desperate furious striding, it is a kind of pleading.
With you, evil and good really have faces.
With us, it's mostly a struggle between roots, ciphers, and shades of light.

Those who run death's errands don't avoid the daylight.
They rule from glass stories. They swarm in the sun's blaze.
They lean across the counter and turn their head.

Far away I happen to stop before one of the new façades.
Many windows all merging together into one single window.
The light of the night sky is caught there with the gliding of the treetops.
It is a mirroring sea without waves, erect in the summer night.

Violence seems unreal
for a little.

3

The sun scorches. The plane flies low
throwing a shadow in the form of a large cross rushing forward on the
      ground.
A man is crouching in the field at something.
The shadow comes.
For a fraction of a second he is in the middle of the cross.

I have seen the cross that hangs under cool church vaults.
Sometimes it's like a snapshot
of something in violent movement.

Slow Music

The building is closed. The sun crowds in through the windows
and warms up the surfaces of desks
that are strong enough to take the load of human fate.

We are outside, today, on the long wide slope.
Many wear dark clothes. You can stand in the sun with your eyes shut
and feel yourself being slowly blown forward.

I come down to the water too seldom. But here I am now,
among large stones with peaceful backs.
Stones that slowly migrated backward up out of the waves.

SEEING IN THE DARK

MÖRKERSEENDE

1970

The Name

I grow sleepy during the car journey and I drive in under the trees at the side of the road. I curl up in the back seat and sleep. For how long? Hours. Darkness has fallen.

Suddenly I'm awake and don't know where I am. Wide-awake, but it doesn't help. Where am I? WHO am I? I am something that wakens in a backseat, twists about in panic like a cat in a sack. Who?

At last my life returns. My name appears like an angel. Outside the walls a trumpet signal blows (as in the *Leonora* Overture) and the rescuing footsteps come smartly down the overlong stairway. It is I! It is I!

But impossible to forget the fifteen-second struggle in the hell of oblivion, a few meters from the main road, where the traffic glides past with its lights on.

A Few Minutes

The squat pine in the swamp holds up its crown: a dark rag.
But what you see is nothing
compared to the roots, the widespread, secretly creeping, immortal or
        half-mortal
root system.

I you she he also branch out.
Outside what one wills.
Outside the Metropolis.

A shower falls out of the milk-white summer sky.
It feels as if my five senses were linked to another creature
that moves stubbornly
as the brightly clad runners in a stadium where the darkness streams
        down.

Breathing Space July

The man lying on his back under the high trees
is up there too. He rills out in thousands of twigs,
sways to and fro,
sits in an ejector seat that releases in slow motion.

The man down by the jetties narrows his eyes at the water.
The jetties grow old more quickly than people.
Their timbers are silvery grey, they have stones in their stomach.
The blinding light beats straight in.

The man traveling all day in an open boat
over the glittering straits
will sleep at last inside a blue lamp
while the islands creep like large moths across the glass.

By the River

Talking with contemporaries I saw heard behind their faces
the stream
that flowed and flowed and pulled with it the willing and the unwilling.

And the creature with stuck-together eyes that wants
to go right down the rapids with the current
throws itself forward without trembling
in a furious hunger for simplicity.

The water pulls more and more swiftly

as where the river narrows and flows over
in the rapids—the place where I paused
after a journey through dry woods

one June evening: the radio gives the latest
on the special meeting: Kosygin, Eban.
A few thoughts drill despairingly.
A few people down in the village.

And under the suspension bridge the masses of water hurl
past. Here comes the timber. Some logs
shoot out like torpedoes. Others turn
crosswise, twirl sluggishly and helplessly away

and some nose against the riverbanks,
push among stones and rubbish, wedge fast,
and pile up like clasped hands

motionless in the uproar . . .

                           I saw heard from the bridge
in a cloud of mosquitoes,
together with some boys. Their bicycles
buried in the greenery—only the horns
stuck out.

Outskirts

Men in overalls the same color as the earth come up out of a ditch.
It is an intermediate place, stalemate, neither city nor country.
The high cranes on the horizon want to take the great leap but the
          clocks don't want to.
Cement pipes, scattered around, lick up the light with dry tongues.
Auto body repair shops in former barns.
The stones throw their shadows abruptly like objects on the surface of
          the moon.
And these places just multiply.
Like what they bought with Judas's money: "the potter's field, to bury
          strangers in."

Traffic

The long-distance truck with its trailer crawls through the mist
and is a large shadow of the dragonfly larva
that stirs in the mud of the lake bed.

Headlights meet in a dripping forest.
One can't see the other's face.
The flood of light pours through the needles.

We come shadows vehicles from all directions
in the twilight, drive together behind each other
past each other, glide forward in a muffled clamor

out onto the plain where factories brood
and the buildings sink two millimeters
each year—the ground is eating them slowly.

Unidentified paws set their marks
on the brightest products dreamt up here.
The seeds try to live in the asphalt.

But first the chestnut trees, gloomy as if
they prepared a blossoming of iron gloves
instead of white clusters, and behind them

the company office—a faulty strip-light
blinks blinks. There's a secret door here. Unlock it—
look into the inverted periscope

downward, to the openings, to the deep tubes
where the algae grow like the beards of the dead
and the Cleaner drifts in his dress of slime

with feebler and feebler strokes, on the point of suffocating.
And no one knows what will happen, only that the chain
perpetually breaks, perpetually joins together again.

Night Duty

1

Tonight I am down among the ballast.
I am one of the silent weights
that prevent the ship from overturning!
Obscure faces in the darkness like stones.
They can only hiss: "Don't touch me."

2

Other voices throng, the listener
glides like a lean shadow over the radio's
luminous band of stations.
The language marches in step with the executioners.
Therefore we must get a new language.

3

The wolf is here, friend for every hour
touching the windows with his tongue.
The valley is full of crawling axe handles.
The night-flier's din pours over the sky
sluggishly, like a wheelchair with iron rims.

4

They are digging up the town. But it is silent now.
Under the elms in the churchyard:
an empty excavator. The scoop against the earth—
the gesture of a man who has fallen asleep at the table
with his fist in front of him. —Bell-ringing.

The Open Window

I stood shaving one morning
before the open window
one story up.
I switched the razor on.
It began to purr.
It buzzed louder and louder.
It grew to an uproar.
It grew to a helicopter
and a voice—the pilot's—penetrated
through the din, shrieked:
"Keep your eyes open!
You're seeing all this for the last time."
We rose.
Flew low over the summer.
So many things I liked, have they any weight?
Dozens of dialects of green.
And especially the red of the wooden house walls.
The beetles glistened in the dung, in the sun.
Cellars that were pulled up by the roots
flew through the air.
Activity.
The printing presses crawled.
Just now the people were
the only things that were still.
They observed a minute's silence.
And especially the dead in the country churchyard
were still
as if sitting for a picture during the camera' infancy.
Fly low!
I didn't know where I
turned my head—
with a double field of vision
like a horse.

Preludes

1

I shy at something that comes shuffling crosswise in the sleet.
Fragment of what will happen.
A wall broken loose. Something without eyes. Hard.
A face of teeth!
A solitary wall. Or is the house there
although I don't see it?
The future: an army of empty houses
picking its way forward in the sleet.

2

Two truths draw nearer each other. One moves from inside, one moves
    from outside
and where they meet we have a chance to see ourselves.

He who notices what is happening cries despairingly: "Stop!
Whatever you like, if only I avoid knowing myself."

And there is a boat that wants to put in—it tries just here—
thousands of times it comes and tries.

Out of the forest gloom comes a long boat hook, it is pushed in through
    the open window,
in among the party guests who danced themselves warm.

3

The apartment where I lived the greater part of my life is to be cleared out. It is now quite empty. The anchor has let go—although we are still mourning it is the lightest apartment in the whole city. The truth needs no furniture. I have made a journey around life and have returned to the starting point: a blown-out room. Things I have been a part of here appear on the walls like Egyptian paintings, scenes on the inside of a burial chamber. But they are steadily being erased. For the light is too strong. The windows have become bigger. The empty apartment is a large telescope aimed at the sky. It is as silent as a Quaker service. What can be heard are the backyard pigeons, their cooing.

Upright

In a moment of concentration I succeeded in catching the hen, I stood with it in my hands. Curiously, it did not feel properly alive: stiff, dry, an old white feather-trimmed woman's hat, which cried out truths from 1912. Thunder hung in the air. From the wooden plank, a scent rose as when you open a photo album so aged that you can no longer identify the portraits.

I carried the hen into the enclosure and let her go. Suddenly she was very much alive, knew where she was, and ran according to the rules. The hen-yard is full of taboos. But the earth around is full of love and tenacity. A low stone wall half overgrown with greenery. As dusk falls the stones begin to gleam faintly with the hundred-year-old warmth of the hands that shaped them.

The winter has been hard, but now summer is here and the earth wants to have us upright. Free but wary, as when you stand up in a slim boat. A memory of Africa is wakened in me: on the shore at Chari, many boats, a very friendly atmosphere, the almost blue-black people with three parallel scars on each cheek (the Sara tribe). I am welcomed aboard—a canoe of dark wood. It is surprisingly rickety, even when I squat. A balancing act. If the heart lies on the left side you must incline your head a little to the right, nothing in the pockets, no large gestures, all rhetoric must be left behind. Just this: rhetoric is impossible here. The canoe glides out on the water.

The Bookcase

It was fetched from the dead woman's apartment. It stood empty for a few days, empty until I filled it with books, all the bound ones, the heavy ones. In doing so, I let in the netherworld. Something rose from underneath, slowly and inexorably like a massive column of mercury. Your head couldn't turn away.

The dark volumes, closed faces. They are like Algerians who stood at the Friedrichstrasse checkpoint and waited for the Volkspolizei to examine their passports. My own passport has long since lain among the glass cages. And the haze of Berlin in those days is also inside the bookcase. An old despair tastes of Passchendaele and the Versailles Peace, tastes even older. The dark heavy tomes—I come back to them—are in reality a kind of passport, thick from having collected so many stamps through the centuries. Evidently you cannot travel with enough heavy baggage, now when you set off, when you at last . . .

All the old historians are there, they rise up and look into our family. Nothing is heard but their lips are always moving behind the glass ("Passchendaele . . ."). It makes you think of an aged civil service department (a pure ghost story follows), a building where portraits of long-since-dead men hang behind glass until one morning vapor appears inside the glass. They began to breathe during the night.

The bookcase is still more powerful. The glances straight across the border! A gleaming membrane, the gleaming membrane on a dark river the room must see itself in. And you cannot turn your head away.

PATHS

STIGAR

1973

To Friends Behind a Frontier

1

I wrote so meagerly to you. But what I couldn't write
swelled and swelled like an old-fashioned airship
and drifted away at last through the night sky.

2

The letter is now at the censor's. He lights his lamp.
In the glare my words fly up like monkeys on a grille,
rattle it, stop, and bare their teeth.

3

Read between the lines. We'll meet in 200 years
when the microphones in the hotel walls are forgotten
and can at last sleep, become trilobites.

From the Thaw of 1966

Headlong headlong waters; roaring; old hypnosis.
The river swamps the car cemetery, glitters
behind the masks.
I hold tight to the bridge railing.
The bridge: a big iron bird sailing past death.

Sketch in October

The tugboat is freckled with rust. What's it doing here so far inland?
It's a heavy extinguished lamp in the cold.
But the trees have wild colors: signals to the other shore.
As if someone wanted to be fetched.

On my way home I see mushrooms sprouting through the grass.
They are the fingers, stretching for help, of someone
who has long been sobbing alone down in the darkness.
We are the earth's.

Further In

On the main road into the city
when the sun is low.
The traffic thickens, crawls.
It is a sluggish dragon glittering.
I am one of the dragon's scales.
Suddenly the red sun is
right in the middle of the windshield
streaming in.
I am transparent
and writing becomes visible
inside me
words in invisible ink
that appear
when the paper is held to the fire!
I know I must get far away
straight through the city and then
further until it is time to go out
and walk far into the forest.
Walk in the footprints of the badger.
It gets dark, difficult to see.
In there on the moss lie stones.
One of the stones is precious.
It can change everything
it can make the darkness shine.
It is a switch for the whole country.
Everything depends on it.
Look at it, touch it . . .

The Outpost

I'm ordered out to a heap of stones
like a distinguished corpse from the Iron Age.
The others are back in the tent sleeping
stretched out like spokes in a wheel.

In the tent the stove rules: a big snake
that has swallowed a ball of fire and hisses.
But out in the spring night it is silent
among cold stones waiting for day.

Out in the cold I begin to fly
like a shaman, I fly to her body
with its white marks from her bikini—
we were out in the sun. The moss was warm.

I flit over warm moments
but can't stop for long.
They're whistling me back through space—
I crawl out from the stones. Here and now.

Mission: to be where I am.
Even in that ridiculous, deadly serious
role—I am the place
where creation is working itself out.

Daybreak, the sparse tree trunks
are colored now, the frostbitten
spring flowers form a silent search party
for someone who has vanished in the dark.

But to be where I am. And to wait.
I am anxious, stubborn, confused.
Coming events, they're there already!
I know it. They're outside:

a murmuring crowd outside the gate.
They can pass only one by one.
They want in. Why? They're coming
one by one. I am the turnstile.

Along the Radius

1

The ice-bound river is blazing with sun
here is the world's roof
silence.

I'm sitting on an upturned boat on the bank
swallowing the drug of silence
spinning gently.

2

A wheel spreads out endlessly, turns.
Here is the center, almost
still.

Further out, perceptible movement: the steps in the snow
the writing which shuffles along
the façades.

The rumbling traffic on the highways
and the silent traffic
of ghosts.

And further out: the tragic masks in the headwind
in the whine of speed—further out:
the rush

where the last words of love evaporate—
the drips that creep
on the steel wings—

profiles that cry out—the suspended headphones
chatter at each other—
kamikaze!

3

The ice-bound river glitters and is silent.
The shadows lie deep
and voiceless.

My steps were explosions in the ground
that the silence paints over
paints over.

Looking Through the Ground

The white sun is soaking through the smog.
The light drips, gropes its way down

to my deep-down eyes that are resting
deep under the city looking up

seeing the city from below: streets, foundations—
like aerial photos of a city in war

the wrong way around—a mole photo:
silent squares in somber colors.

The decisions are taken there. No telling
bones of the dead from bones of the living.

The sunlight's volume is turned up,
it floods into flight cabins and peapods.

December Evening 1972

Here I come, the invisible man, perhaps employed
by a Great Memory to live right now. And I am driving past

the locked-up white church—a wooden saint stands
smiling, helpless, as if they had taken away his glasses.

He is alone. Everything else is now, now, now. The law of gravity presses
       us
against our work by day and against our beds by night. The war.

The Dispersed Congregation

1

We made an effort, showing our homes.
The visitor thought: you live well.
The slum is within you.

2

Inside the church: vaults and columns
white as plaster, like the plaster bandage
around the broken arm of faith.

3

Inside the church: the begging bowl
that raises itself from the floor
and passes along the pews.

4

But the church bells must go under the earth.
They hang in the sewage tunnels.
They toll under our steps.

5

The sleepwalker Nicodemus on his way
to the Address. Who has the address?
Don't know. But that's where we're going.

Late May

Apple trees and cherry trees in bloom help the town soar
in the sweet dirty May night, white life jacket, my thoughts range out.
Grasses and weeds with silent stubborn wingbeats.
The mailbox shines calmly, what's written can't be taken back.

Soft cool wind passes through my shirt and gropes for my heart.
Apple trees and cherry trees, they laugh silently at Solomon,
they blossom in my tunnel. I need them
not to forget but to remember.

Elegy

I open the first door.
It's a large sunlit room.
A heavy car passes in the street
and makes the porcelain tremble.

I open door number two.
Friends! You drank the darkness
and became visible.

Door number three. A narrow hotel room.
Outlook on a back street.
A lamp sparking on the asphalt.
Beautiful slag of experiences.

BALTICS

ÖSTERSJÖAR

1974

Baltics

1

It was before the age of the radio masts.

Grandfather was a new-made pilot. In the almanac he wrote down the
>   vessels he piloted—
names, destinations, drafts.
Examples from 1884:
Steamer Tiger   Capt. Rowan   16 ft   Hull Gefle Furusund
Brigg Ocean   Capt. Andersen   8 ft   Sandöfjord Hernösand Furusund
Steamer St. Petersburg   Capt. Libenberg   11 ft   Stettin Libau Sandhamn

He took them out to the Baltic, through the marvelous labyrinth of
>   islands and waters.
And those who met on board and were carried by the same hull for a
>   few hours, or days,
how much did they come to know one another?
Conversations in misspelled English, understanding and misunderstand-
>   ing but very little conscious falsehood.
How much did they come to know each other?

When it was thick fog: half speed, half blind ahead. At one single stride
>   the cape emerged from the invisible and was right on them.
Every other minute a bellowing signal. His eyes read straight into the
>   invisible.
(Had he the labyrinth in his head?)
The minutes passed.
Shallows and skerries he memorized like psalm verses.
And that feeling of "we're just here" that must be kept, like carrying a
>   brimful pail without spilling a drop.

A glance down in the engine room.
The compound machine long-lived as a human heart toiled with great
>   supple bouncing movements, acrobats of steel, and the smells
>   rose as if from a kitchen.

2

The wind is in the pine forest. Sighing heavily and lightly.
The Baltic is also sighing in the middle of the island, far within the forest
          you are out on the open sea.
The old woman hated the sighing in the trees. Her face stiffened in
          melancholy when the wind picked up:
"We must think about the men out in the boats."
But she heard something else as well in the sighing, as I do, we are kin.
(We are walking together. She's been dead for thirty years.)
There's sighing, yes and no, understanding and misunderstanding.
There's sighing, three sound children, one in a sanatorium and two dead.
The great current that blows life into some flames and blows others out.
          The conditions.
Sighing: Save me, O God; for the waters are come in unto my soul.
You go on, listening, and then reach a point where the frontiers open
or rather
where everything becomes a frontier. An open place sunk in darkness.
          The people stream out from the faintly lit buildings. Murmuring.

A new breath of wind and the place lies desolate and silent again.
A new breath of wind, sighing about other shores.
It's about war.
It's about places where citizens are under control,
where their thoughts are made with emergency exits,
where a conversation between friends really becomes a test of what
          friendship means.
And when you are with people you don't know so well. Control. A certain
          sincerity is in place
if only you don't take your eyes off what's drifting on the outskirts of the
          conversation: something dark, a dark stain.
Something that can drift in
and destroy everything. Don't take your eyes off it!
What can we compare it to? A mine?
No, that would be too concrete. And almost too peaceful—for on our
          coast most of the stories about mines have a happy ending, the
          terror short-lived.

As in this story from the lightship: "In the autumn of 1915 we slept
      uneasily . . ." etc. A drift-mine was sighted
as it drifted slowly toward the lightship, then sank and resurfaced, some-
      times hidden by the waters, sometimes glimpsed like a spy in a
      crowd.
The crew was in a sweat and shot at it with rifles. No use. At last they put
      out a boat and made fast a long line to it and slowly and carefully
      towed it to the experts.
Afterward they set up the dark shell of the mine in a sandy plantation as
      an ornament
together with the shells of Strombus Gigas from the West Indies.

And the sea wind is in the dry pines further away, hurrying over the
      churchyard sand,
past the leaning stones, the pilots' names.
The dry sighing
of great doors opening and great doors closing.

3

In the half-dark corner of a Gotland church, in a glimmer of soft mildew
there's a sandstone font—12th century—the mason's name
is still visible, shines out
like a row of teeth in a mass grave:
                    HEGWALDR
                            the name's left. And his pictures
here and on the sides of other pots, human swarms, figures stepping out
            of the stone.
There the eyes' kernels of good and evil are split.
Herod at table: the roasted cock flies up and crows "Christus natus
            est"—the waiter was executed—
close by, the child is born, under clusters of faces dignified and helpless
            as those of young apes.
And the fleeing steps of the pious
echoing over dragon-scaled sewer openings.
(The images stronger in memory than when seen direct, strongest
when in memory the font turns like a slow rumbling merry-go-round.)
Nowhere lee. Everywhere risk.
As it was. As it is.
Only in there is there peace, in the vessel's water that no one sees,
but on the outer walls the battle is raging.
And peace can come drop by drop, perhaps at night
when we know nothing
or when you are lying in a hospital ward on a drip.

People, beasts, ornaments.
There is no landscape. Ornaments.

Mr. B, my amiable traveling companion, in exile,
released from Robben Island, says:
"I envy you. I feel nothing for nature.
But *figures in a landscape*, that says something to me."

Here are figures in a landscape.
A photo from 1865. The steamer is at the pier in the sound.
Five figures. A lady in a bright crinoline, like a bell, like a flower.
The men are like extras in a rustic play.
They're all beautiful, irresolute, in the process of being rubbed out.
They step ashore for a little while. They're being rubbed out.
The steam launch is an extinct model—
high funnel, sunroof, narrow hull—
it's utterly foreign, a UFO that's landed.
Everything else in the photo is shockingly real:
the ripples on the water,
the opposite shore—
I can stroke my hand over the rough rockfaces,
I can hear the sighing in the spruces.
It's near. It's
today.
The waves are topical.

Now a hundred years later. The waves are coming in from no-man's water
and break on the stones.
I walk along the shore. Walking along the shore is not as it was.
You have to take in too much, keep up many conversations at once, you
       have thin walls.
Each thing has acquired a new shadow behind the usual shadow
and you hear it trailing along even in total darkness.

It's night.

The strategic planetarium rotates. The lenses stare in the dark.
The night sky is full of numbers and they are fed
into a twinkling cupboard,
a piece of furniture
where there lives the energy of a locust swarm that denudes the acreage
       of Somaliland in half an hour.

I don't know if we are at the beginning or coming to the end.
The summing up can't be done, the summing up is impossible.
The summing up is the mandrake—
(See the encyclopedia of superstitions:

MANDRAKE

miracle-working plant
which when torn out of the ground gave off such an appalling scream
a man would drop dead. A dog had to do it.)

4

From leeward,
closeups.

Bladderwrack. The weed-forests shine in the clear water, they are young,
you want to emigrate there, lie down full-length on your mirror
image and sink to a certain depth—the weed that holds itself up
with air bladders as we hold ourselves up with ideas.

Bullhead. The fish who is a toad who wanted to become a butterfly and
succeeded a third of the way, hides himself in the seaweed but is
drawn up in the nets, hooked fast by his pathetic spikes and
warts—when you disentangle it from the meshes your hands
gleam with slime.

Rockface. Out on the sun-warmed lichens the insects scurry, they're in a
rush like second hands—the pine throws a shadow, it moves
slowly like an hour hand—inside me time stands still, an infinity
of time, the time required to forget all languages and to invent
perpetuum mobile.

On the lee side you can hear the grass growing: a faint drumming from
underneath, a faint roar of millions of little gas flames, that's
what it's like to hear the grass growing.

And now: the width of water, without doors, the open frontier
that grows broader and broader
the further out you reach.

There are days when the Baltic is a calm endless roof.
Then dream your naïve dreams about someone crawling on the roof try-
ing to sort out the flag-lines,
trying to hoist
the rag—

the flag that is so eroded by the wind and blackened by the funnels and
bleached by the sun it can be everyone's.

But it's a long way to Liepaja.

5

July 30th. The strait has become eccentric—swarming with jellyfish to-
day for the first time in years, they pump themselves forward
calmly and patiently, they belong to the same line: *Aurelia*, they
drift like flowers after a sea burial, if you take them out of the wa-
ter their entire form vanishes, as when an indescribable truth is
lifted out of silence and formulated into an inert mass, but they
are untranslatable, they must stay in their own element.

August 2nd. Something wants to be said but the words don't agree.
Something which can't be said,
aphasia,
there are no words but perhaps a style . . .

You can wake up in the small hours
jot down a few words
on the nearest paper, a newsprint margin
(the words radiate meaning!)
but in the morning: the same words now say nothing, scrawls, slips of
the tongue.
Or fragments of the high nocturnal style that drew past?

Music comes to a man, he's a composer, he's played, makes a career,
becomes Conservatory Director.
The climate changes, he's condemned by the authorities.
His pupil K is set up as prosecutor.
He's threatened, degraded, removed.
After a few years the disgrace lessens, he's rehabilitated.
Then, cerebral hemorrhage: paralysis on the right side with aphasia, can
grasp only short phrases, says the wrong words.
Beyond the reach of eulogy or execration.
But the music's left, he keeps composing in his own style,
for the rest of his days he becomes a medical sensation.

He wrote music to texts he no longer understood—
in the same way
we express something through our lives
in the humming chorus full of mistaken words.

The death-lectures went on for several terms. I attended
together with people I didn't know
(who are you?)
—then each went his own way, profiles.

I looked at the sky and at the earth and straight ahead
and since then I've been writing a long letter to the dead
on a typewriter with no ribbon just a horizon line
so the words knock in vain and nothing sticks.

I pause with my hand on the door handle, take the pulse of the house.
The walls are so full of life
(the children don't dare sleep alone in the little room upstairs—what
        makes me safe makes them uneasy).

August 3rd. In the damp grass
a greeting shuffles from the Middle Ages, the Edible Snail,
subtle gleaming grey-and-yellow, with his house aslant,
introduced by monks who liked their escargots—the Franciscans were
        here,
broke stone and burned lime, the island became theirs in 1288, a gift of
        King Magnus
("Almes fordoth all wykkednes / And quenchyth synne and makyth hyt
        les")
the forest fell, the ovens burned, the lime was shipped in
for the building of the monastery . . .
                                        Sister snail
almost motionless in the grass, the antennae are sucked in
and rolled out, disturbances and hesitation . . .
How like myself in my searching!

The wind that's been blowing carefully all day
—the blades of grass on the outer skerries are all counted—
has lain down peacefully at the heart of the island. The match flame
        stands straight.
The sea painting and the forest painting darken together.
The foliage on the five-story trees turns black.
"Each summer is the last." Empty words
for the creatures in the late-summer midnight
where the crickets whirr their sewing machines frantically
and the Baltic is close
and the lonely water tap rises among the wild roses
like the statue of a horseman. The water tastes of iron.

6

Grandmother's story before it's forgotten: her parents die young
father first. When the widow knows the disease will take her too
she walks from house to house, sails from island to island
with her daughter. "Who can take Maria?" A strange house
on the other side of the bay takes her. There they have the means.
But that didn't make them good. The mask of piety cracks.
Maria's childhood ends too early, she's an unpaid servant
in perpetual coldness. Year after year. Perpetual seasickness
during the long stints of rowing, solemn terror
at table, the looks, the pike-skin scrunching
in her mouth: be grateful, be grateful.

                                                        She never looked back
but because of that she could see what was new
and catch hold of it.
Out of encirclement.

I remember her. I would press close to her
and at the moment of death (the moment of crossing?) she sent out a
            thought
so that I—a five-year-old—understood what happened
half an hour before they rang.

Her I remember. But in the next brown photo
the unknown man—
dated by his clothes to the middle of the last century.
A man around thirty: the vigorous eyebrows,
the face looking straight into my eyes
and whispering: "Here I am."
But who "I" am
there's no one anymore who remembers. No one.

TB? Isolation?

Once coming up from the sea
on the stony slope steaming with grass he stopped
and felt the black bandage on his eyes.

Here, behind dense thickets—is it the island's oldest house?
The low, two-centuries-old fisherman's hut, log-cabin style, with heavy
coarse grey timbers.
And the modern brass padlock has clicked it all together and shines like
the ring in the nose of an old bull
who refuses to get up.
So much wood crouching. On the roof the ancient tiles that have slipped
downways and crossways over each other
(the original pattern deranged over the years by the rotation of the earth)
it reminds me of something . . . I was there . . . wait: it's the old Jewish
cemetery in Prague
where the dead live more packed than they were in life, the stones
packed packed.
So much love encircled! The tiles with their lichen-script in an unknown
tongue
are the stones in the ghetto cemetery of the archipelago folk, the stones
raised and tumbled. —
The hovel is lit up
with all those who were driven by a certain wave, by a certain wind
right out here to their fates.

THE TRUTHBARRIER

SANNINGSBARRIÄREN

1978

· I ·

Citoyens

The night after the accident I dreamt of a pockmarked man
who walked through the alleys singing.
Danton!
Not the other one—Robespierre doesn't take such walks,
Robespierre spends a careful hour each morning on his toilette,
the rest of the day he devotes to The People.
In the paradise of the pamphlets, among the machines of virtue.
Danton—
or the man who wore his mask
seemed to be standing on stilts.
I saw his face from beneath.
Like the scarred moon,
half in light, half in mourning.
I wanted to say something.
A weight in the breast, the plummet
that makes the clocks go,
the hands turn: year 1, year 2 . . .
A sharp scent like sawdust in the tiger stalls.
And—as always in dreams—no sun.
But the walls were shining
in the alleys that curved
down to the waiting room, the curved room,
the waiting room where we all . . .

The Crossing-Place

Ice-wind in my eyes and the suns dance
in the kaleidoscope of tears as I cross
the street that's followed me for so long, the street
where Greenland-summer shines from puddles.

Around me the whole strength of the street swarms,
power that remembers nothing, wants nothing.
For a thousand years, in the earth deep
under traffic the unborn forest quietly waits.

I get the idea that the street can see me.
Its sight is so dim the sun itself
is a grey ball in a black space.
But right now I am shining! The street sees me.

The Clearing

Deep in the forest there's an unexpected clearing that can be reached only by someone who has lost his way.

The clearing is enclosed in a forest that is choking itself. Black trunks with the ashy beard stubble of lichen. The trees are tangled tightly together and are dead right up to the tops, where a few solitary green twigs touch the light. Beneath them: shadow brooding on shadow, and the swamp growing.

But in the open space the grass is unexpectedly green and alive. There are big stones lying here as if they'd been arranged. They must be the foundation stones of a house, but I could be wrong. Who lived here? No one can tell us. The names exist somewhere in an archive that no one opens (only archives stay young). The oral tradition has died and with it the memories. The gypsy people remember but those who have learned to write forget. Write down, and forget.

The homestead murmurs with voices, it is the center of the world. But the inhabitants die or move out, the chronicle breaks off. Desolate for many years. And the homestead becomes a sphinx. At last everything's gone, except the foundation stones.

Somehow I've been here before, but now I must go. I dive in among the thickets. I can push my way through only with one step forward and two to the side, like a chess knight. Bit by bit the forest thins and lightens. My steps get longer. A footpath creeps toward me. I am back in the communications network.

On the humming electricity pole a beetle is sitting in the sun. Beneath the shining wing covers its wings are folded up as ingeniously as a parachute packed by an expert.

How the Late Autumn Night Novel Begins

The ferryboat smells of oil and something rattles all the time like an obsession. The spotlight's turned on. We're pulling into the jetty. I'm the only one who wants off here. "Need the gangway?" No. I take a long tottering stride into the night and stand on the jetty, on the island. I feel wet and unwieldy, a butterfly that just crawled out of its cocoon, the plastic bags in each hand hang like misshapen wings. I turn around and see the boat gliding away with its shining windows, then grope my way toward the house that has been empty for so long. There's no one in any of the other houses. . . . It's good to fall asleep here. I lie on my back and don't know if I'm asleep or awake. Some books I've read pass by like old sailing ships on their way to the Bermuda Triangle to vanish without trace. . . . I hear a hollow sound, an absentminded drumming. An object the wind keeps knocking against something the earth holds still. If the night is not merely an absence of light, if the night really *is* something, then it's that sound. Stethoscope noises form a slow heart, it beats, falls silent for a time, returns. As if the creature were moving in a zigzag across the Frontier. Or someone knocking in a wall, someone who belongs to the other world but was left behind here, knocking, wanting back. Too late. Couldn't get down there, couldn't get up there, couldn't get aboard. . . . The other world is this world too. Next morning I see a sizzling golden-brown branch. A crawling stack of roots. Stones with faces. The forest is full of abandoned monsters that I love.

To Mats and Laila

The Dateline says still between Samoa and Tonga but the Midnightline glides forward over the ocean and the islands and the roofs of cabins. They're asleep on the other side. Here in Värmland it's broad daylight, a day in early summer with a burning sun—I've thrown aside my luggage. A swim in the sky, the air's so blue . . . Then suddenly I see the ridges on the other side of the lake: they are clean-cut. Like the shaved parts of a patient's head before he has a brain operation. It's been there all the time, I haven't seen it until now. Blinkers and a stiff neck . . . The journey continues. The landscape is now full of hatching and lines, like the old engravings where people wandered among hills and mountains that resembled anthills and villages also composed of thousands of strokes. And each man-ant brought his own little stroke to add to the big engraving; there was no proper center but everything was alive. Something else: the figures are small but each has his own face, the engraver has not denied them that—they are no ants. Most of them are simple people though they can write their names. Proteus on the other hand is a modern man who expresses himself fluently in every style, comes with a "straight message" or empty flourishes depending on which gang he belongs to at that moment. He can't write his name. He shies away from it like a werewolf from a silver bullet. They don't ask for it either, the hydra of the Company or the hydra of the State. . . . The journey continues. In this house lives a man who became desperate one evening and shot at the empty hammock swaying above the grass. And the Midnightline comes closer; it'll soon have covered half its course. (And don't make out I want to turn the clock back.) Tiredness will stream in through the hole left by the sun. . . . For me it's never happened that the diamond of a certain moment cut an indelible score across the world-picture. No, it was wear and tear that rubbed out the bright strange smile. But something's in the process of becoming visible again, it's being worn *in*, begins to look like a smile, no one knows what it's worth. Unaccounted for. Someone catches at my arm each time I try to write.

From the Winter of 1947

Days at school, that muffled thronging fortress.
At dusk I walked home under the shop signs.
Then the whispering without lips: "Wake up, sleepwalker!"
And every object pointed to The Room.

Fifth floor, a view of the yard. The lamp burned
in a circle of terror night after night.
I sat in bed without eyelids, saw filmstrips
filmstrips with the thoughts of insane people.

As if it were necessary . . .
As if the last childhood were being broken up
to make it pass through the grid.
As if it were necessary . . .

I read in books of glass but saw only the other:
the stains pushing through the wallpaper.
It was the living dead
who wanted their portraits painted. . . .

Till dawn when the trashmen came
clattering the metal cans below.
The backyard's peaceful grey bells
ringing me to sleep.

· II ·

Schubertiana

1

In the evening darkness in a place outside New York, a viewpoint where
   one single glance will encompass the homes of eight million
   people.
The giant city becomes a long shimmering drift, a spiral galaxy seen
   from the side.
Within the galaxy coffee cups are pushed across the counter, the shop
   windows beg from passersby, a flurry of shoes leave no prints.
The climbing fire escapes, elevator doors glide shut, behind police-
   locked doors a perpetual seethe of voices.
Slouched bodies doze in subway cars, the hurtling catacombs.
I know too—without statistics—that right now Schubert is being played
   in a room over there and that for someone the notes are more
   real than anything else.

2

The endless expanses of the human brain are crumpled to the size of a fist.
In April the swallow returns to last year's nest under the guttering of this
   very barn in this very parish.
She flies from Transvaal, passes the equator, flies for six weeks over two
   continents, makes for precisely this vanishing dot in the land-
   mass.
And the man who catches the signals from a whole life in a few ordinary
   chords for five strings,
who makes a river flow through the eye of a needle,
is a stout young gentleman from Vienna known to his friends as "The
   Mushroom," who slept with his glasses on
and stood at his writing desk punctually in the morning.
And then the wonderful centipedes of his manuscript were set in motion.

3

The string quintet is playing. I walk home through warm forests with the
    ground springy under me,
curl up like an embryo, fall asleep, roll weightless into the future, suddenly
    feel that the plants have thoughts.

4

So much we have to trust, simply to live through our daily day without
    sinking through the earth!
Trust the piled snow clinging to the mountain slope above the village.
Trust the promises of silence and the smile of understanding, trust that
    the accident telegram isn't for us and that the sudden axe-blow
    from within won't come.
Trust the axles that carry us on the highway in the middle of the three
    hundred times life-size bee-swarm of steel.
But none of this is really worth our confidence.
The five strings say we can trust something else. And they keep us com-
    pany part of the way.
As when the time-switch clicks off in the stairwell and the fingers—
    trustingly—follow the blind handrail that finds its way in the
    darkness.

5

We squeeze together at the piano and play with four hands in F minor,
    two coachmen on the same coach, it looks a little ridiculous.
The hands seem to be moving resonant weights to and fro, as if we were
    tampering with the counterweights
in an effort to disturb the great scale arm's terrible balance: joy and
    suffering weighing exactly the same.
Annie said, "This music is so heroic," and she's right.
But those whose eyes enviously follow men of action, who secretly
    despise themselves for not being murderers,

don't recognize themselves here,
and the many who buy and sell people and believe that everyone can be
bought, don't recognize themselves here.
Not their music. The long melody that remains itself in all its transfor-
mations, sometimes glittering and pliant, sometimes rugged
and strong, snail track and steel wire.
The perpetual humming that follows us—now—
up
the depths.

• III •

The Gallery

I stayed overnight at a motel by the E3.
In my room a smell I'd felt before
in the Asiatic halls of a museum:

masks Tibetan Japanese on a pale wall.

But it's not masks now, it's faces

forcing through the white wall of oblivion
to breathe, to ask about something.
I lie awake watching them struggle
and disappear and return.

Some lend each other features, exchange faces
far inside me
where oblivion and memory wheel and deal.

They force through oblivion's second coat
the white wall
they fade out fade in.

Here is a sorrow that doesn't call itself sorrow.

Welcome to the authentic galleries!
Welcome to the authentic galleys!
The authentic grilles!

The karate boy who paralyzed someone
is still dreaming of fast money.

This woman keeps buying things
to toss in the hungry mouth of the vacuum
sneaking up behind her.

Mr. X doesn't dare go out.
A dark stockade of ambiguous people
stands between him
and the steadily retreating horizon.

She who once fled from Karelia
she who could laugh . . .
now shows herself
but dumb, petrified, a statue from Sumer.

As when I was ten and came home late.
In the stairwell the light switched off
but the lift I stood in was bright, it rose
like a diving-bell through black depths
floor by floor while imagined faces
pressed against the grille . . .

But the faces are not imagined now, they are real.

I lie straight out like a cross street.

Many step out from the white mist.
We touched each other once—we did!

A long bright carbolic-scented corridor.
The wheelchair. The teenage girl
learning to talk after the car crash.

He who tried to call out underwater
and the world's cold mass poured in
through nose and mouth.

Voices in the microphone said: Speed is power,
speed is power!
Play the game, the show must go on!

We move through our career stiffly, step by step,
as if in a Noh drama—

masks, high-pitched song: It's me, it's me!
The one who's failed
is represented by a rolled-up blanket.

An artist said: Before, I was a planet
with its own dense atmosphere.
Entering rays were broken into rainbows.
Perpetual raging thunderstorms, within.

Now I'm extinct and dry and open.
I no longer have childlike energy.
I have a hot side and a cold side.

No rainbows.

I stayed overnight in the echoing house.
Many want to come in through the walls
but most of them can't make it:

they're overcome by the white hiss of oblivion.

Anonymous singing drowns in the walls.
Discreet tappings that don't want to be heard
drawn-out sighs
my old repartees creeping homelessly.

Listen to society's mechanical self-reproaches
the voice of the big fan
like the artificial wind in mine tunnels
six hundred meters down.

Our eyes keep wide open under the bandages.

If I could at least make them realize
that this trembling beneath us
means we are on a bridge.

Often I have to stand motionless.
I am the knife thrower's partner at a circus!
Questions I tossed aside in rage
come whining back

don't hit me, but nail down my shape
my rough outline
and stay in place when I've walked away.

Often I have to be silent. Voluntarily!
Because "the last word" is said again and again.
Because good-day and good-bye . . .
Because this very day . . .

Because the margins rise at last
over their brims
and flood the text.

I stayed overnight at the sleepwalker's motel.
Many faces here are desperate
others smoothed out
after the pilgrim's walk through oblivion.

They breathe vanish struggle back again.
They look past me.
They all want to reach the icon of justice.

It happens rarely
that one of us really *sees* the other:

a person shows himself for an instant
as in a photograph but clearer
and in the background
something that is bigger than his shadow.

He's standing full-length before a mountain.
It's more a snail's shell than a mountain.
It's more a house than a snail's shell.
It's not a house but has many rooms.
It's indistinct but overwhelming.
He grows out of it, it out of him.
It's his life, it's his labyrinth.

· IV ·

Below Zero

We are at a party that doesn't love us. At last the party lets its mask drop and shows itself for what it really is: a marshalling yard. Cold colossi stand on rails in the mist. Chalk scribbled on the wagon doors.

It shouldn't be said but there is much suppressed violence here. That's why the components are so heavy. And why it's so hard to see something else, too: a little reflection from a mirror, flitting on the house-walls and gliding through the unknowing forest of glimmering faces, a biblical text that was never written: "Come unto me, for I am full of contradictions, like you."

Tomorrow I am working in another town. I swish toward it through the morning hour, which is like a big dark-blue cylinder. Orion hangs above the ground-frost. Children are standing in a silent cluster waiting for the school bus, children no one prays for. The light is growing as slowly as our hair.

The Boat—The Village

A Portuguese fishing boat, blue, the wash rolls up the Atlantic a little.
A blue speck far out, but still I'm there, the six aboard don't notice we're
    seven.

I saw such a boat being built, it lay like a big lute without strings
in Poor Valley, the village where they wash and wash in fury, patience,
    melancholy.

The shore black with people, some meeting breaking up, the loudspeak-
    ers being carried away.
Soldiers led the speaker's Mercedes through the crush, words drummed
    on its metal sides.

The Black Mountains

At the next bend the bus broke free of the mountain's cold shadow,
turned its nose to the sun, and crept roaring upward.
We were packed in. The dictator's bust was
wrapped in newspaper. A bottle passed from mouth to mouth.
Death, the birthmark, was growing on all of us, quicker on some, slower
        on others.
Up in the mountains the blue sea caught up with the sky.

Homeward

A telephone call ran out in the night and glittered over the countryside
        and in the suburbs.
Afterward I slept uneasily in the hotel bed.
I was like the needle in a compass carried through the forest by an orien-
        teer with a thumping heart.

After a Long Drought

The summer evening is grey.
The rain steals down from the sky
and lands quietly as if
it had to overpower someone sleeping.

The water rings jostle on the bay's surface
and that is the only surface there is—
the other is height and depth
soar and sink.

Two pine stems
shoot up and end in long hollow signal drums.
Gone are the cities and the sun.
The thunder's in the tall grass.

It's possible to ring up the mirage island.
It's possible to hear the grey voice.
Iron ore is honey for the thunder.
It's possible to live with one's code.

A Place in the Forest

On the way there a pair of startled wings clattered up—that was all. You
go alone. A tall building that consists entirely of cracks, a building that is
perpetually tottering but can never collapse. The thousandfold sun floats
in through the cracks. In this play of light an inverted law of gravity pre-
vails: the house is anchored in the sky and whatever falls, falls upward.
There you can turn around. There you are allowed to grieve. You can dare
to face certain old truths otherwise kept packed, in storage. The roles I
have, deep down, float up, hang like the dried skulls in the ancestral cabin
on some out-of-the-way Melanesian islet. A childlike aura circles the
gruesome trophies. So mild it is, in the forest.

Funchal

The fish restaurant on the beach, simple, a shack built by shipwrecked people. Many turn away at the door, but not the gusts from the sea. A shadow stands in his reeking cabin frying two fish according to an old recipe from Atlantis—small explosion of garlic, oil spills over the tomato slices. Every bite says that the ocean wishes us well, a humming from the deep.

She and I look into each other. Like climbing up the wild blossoming hillsides without feeling the least tiredness. We're on the side of the animals, we're welcome, we don't get older. But over the years we've experienced so much together. We remember that, and also times when we were good for nothing (as when we lined up to give blood to the flourishing giant—he had ordered transfusions), things that would've separated us if they hadn't brought us closer, and things we forgot together—but they have not forgotten us. They've become stones, dark ones and light ones. Stones in a scattered mosaic. And now it happens: the bits fly together, the mosaic is visible. It's waiting for us. It's shining from the wall in our hotel room, a design both violent and tender, perhaps a face, we haven't time to notice everything as we pull off our clothes. . . .

At dusk we go out. The cape's enormous dark blue paw lies sprawled in the sea. We step into the human whirlpool, pushed around in a friendly way, soft controls, everyone chattering in that foreign language. "No man is an island." We become stronger through them, and through ourselves. Through that within us which the other can't see. Which can meet only itself. The innermost paradox, the garage flower, the ventilator to the good darkness. A drink that bubbles in empty glasses. A loudspeaker that sends out silence. A pathway that overgrows again behind each step. A book that can be read only in the dark.

THE WILD MARKET SQUARE

DET VILDA TORGET

1983

• I •

Brief Pause in the Organ Recital

The organ stops playing and the church becomes deathly quiet, but only
      for a couple of seconds.
And the faint rumbling penetrates from the traffic outside, that greater
      organ.

For we are surrounded by the murmuring of the traffic, it flows along
      the cathedral walls.
The outer world glides like a transparent film and with shadows strug-
      gling pianissimo.

And as if it were part of the street noise I hear my pulse beating in the
      silence,
I hear my blood circulating, the cascade that hides inside me, that I walk
      around with,

and as close as my blood and as far away as a memory from when I was
      four
I hear the truck that rumbles past and makes the six-hundred-year-old
      walls tremble.

This could hardly be less like a mother's lap, yet at the moment I am a
      child,
hearing the grown-ups talking far away, the voices of the winners and
      the losers mingling.

On the blue benches a sparse congregation. And the pillars rise like
      strange trees:
no roots (only the common floor) and no crown (only the common roof).

I relive a dream. That I'm standing alone in a churchyard. Everywhere
      heather glows
as far as the eye can reach. Who am I waiting for? A friend. Why doesn't
      he come. He's here already.

Slowly death turns up the lights from underneath, from the ground. The
        heath shines, a stronger and stronger purple—
no, a color no one has seen . . . until the morning's pale light whines in
        through the eyelids

and I wake to that unshakeable PERHAPS that carries me through the
        wavering world.
And each abstract picture of the world is as impossible as the blueprint
        of a storm.

At home stood the all-knowing Encyclopedia, a yard of bookshelf, in it I
        learned to read.
But each one of us has his own encyclopedia written, it grows out of
        each soul,

it's written from birth on, the hundreds of thousands of pages stand
        pressed against each other
and yet with air between them! Like the quivering leaves in a forest. The
        book of contradictions.

What's in it changes by the hour, the pictures retouch themselves, the
        words flicker.
A wake washes through the whole text, followed by the next wave, and
        then the next . . .

From March 1979

Weary of all who come with words, words but no language
I make my way to the snow-covered island.
The untamed has no words.
The unwritten pages spread out on every side!
I come upon the tracks of deer in the snow.
Language but no words.

Memories Look at Me

A June morning, too soon to wake,
too late to fall asleep again.

I must go out—the greenery is dense
with memories, they follow me with their gaze.

They can't be seen, they merge completely into
the background, true chameleons.

They are so close that I can hear them breathe
though the birdsong is deafening.

Winter's Gaze

I lean like a ladder and with my face
reach in to the second floor of the cherry tree.
I'm inside the bell of colors, it chimes with sunlight.
I polish off the swarthy red berries faster than four magpies.

A sudden chill, from a great distance, meets me.
The moment blackens
and remains like an axe-cut in a tree trunk.

From now on it's late. We make off half running
out of sight, down, down into the ancient sewage system.
The tunnels. We wander around for months
half in service and half in flight.

Brief devotions when some hatchway opens above us
and a weak light falls.
We look up: the starry sky through the grating.

The Station

A train has just rolled in. Coach after coach stand still,
but no doors open, no one gets off or on.
Are there no doors at all? Inside, a crowd
of shut-in figures stirring to and fro.
Gazing out through immovable windowpanes.
Outside, a man who walks along the coaches with a hammer.
He strikes the wheels, a feeble clang. Except for here!
Here the chime swells unbelievably: a lightning stroke,
peal of cathedral bells, a sailing-around-the-world peal
that lifts the whole train and the landscape's wet stones.
Everything is singing. This you will remember. Travel on!

• II •

Answers to Letters

In the bottom drawer of my desk I found a letter that first arrived twenty-six years ago. A letter in panic, and it's still breathing when it arrives the second time.

A house has five windows: through four of them the day shines clear and still. The fifth faces a black sky, thunder and storm. I stand at the fifth window. The letter.

Sometimes an abyss opens between Tuesday and Wednesday but twenty-six years could pass in a moment. Time is not a straight line, it's more of a labyrinth, and if you press close to the wall at the right place you can hear the hurrying steps and the voices, you can hear yourself walking past on the other side.

Was the letter ever answered? I don't remember, it *was* long ago. The countless thresholds of the sea kept migrating. The heart kept leaping from second to second like a toad in the wet grass of an August night.

The unanswered letters pile up, like cirrostratus clouds promising bad weather. They make the sunbeams lusterless. One day I will answer. One day when I am dead and can at last concentrate. Or at least so far away from here that I can find myself again. When I'm walking, newly arrived, in the big city, on 125th Street, in the wind on the street of dancing garbage. I who love to stray off and vanish in the crowd, a capital T in the endless mass of the text.

Icelandic Hurricane

Not earth-tremor but sky-quake. Turner could have painted it, lashed tight. A solitary mitten has just whirled by, several miles from its hand. I am going to make my way against the wind to that house on the other side of the field. I flutter in the hurricane. I am x-rayed, the skeleton hands in its resignation. Panic grows as I beat upwind, I founder, I founder and drown on dry land! How heavy everything I suddenly have to drag along, how heavy for the butterfly to tow a barge! There at last. A final wrestle with the door. And now inside. And now inside. Behind the big glass pane. What a strange and wonderful invention glass is—to be close yet untouched. . . . Outside, a horde of transparent sprinters in giant format charges across the lava plain. But I'm no longer fluttering. I'm sitting behind the glass, at rest, my own portrait.

The Blue Wind-Flowers

To be spellbound—nothing's easier. It's one of the oldest tricks of the soil and springtime: the blue wind-flowers. They are in a way unexpected. They shoot up out of the brown rustle of last year in overlooked places where one's gaze never pauses. They glimmer and float—yes, float—from their color. The sharp violet-blue now weighs nothing. Here is ecstasy, but low voiced. "Career"— irrelevant! "Power" and "publicity"—ridiculous! They must have given a great reception up in Nineveh, with pompe and "Trompe up!" Raising the rafters. And above all those brows the crowning crystal chandeliers hung like glass vultures. Instead of such an over-decorated and strident cul-de-sac, the wind-flowers open a secret passage to the real celebration, quiet as death.

The Blue House

It is a night of radiant sun. I stand in the dense forest and look away toward my house with its haze-blue walls. As if I had just died and was seeing the house from a new angle.

It has stood for more than eighty summers. Its wood is impregnated with four times joy and three times sorrow. When someone who lived in the house dies, it is repainted. The dead person himself is painting, without a brush, from inside.

Beyond the house, open ground. Once a garden, now grown over. Stationary breakers of weed, pagodas of weed, welling text, Upanishads of weed, a viking fleet of weed, dragon heads, lances, a weed empire!

Across the overgrown garden flutters the shadow of a boomerang that is thrown again and again. It has something to do with a person who lived in the house long before my time. Almost a child. An impulse comes from him, a thought, a thought like an act of will: "make . . . draw . . ." To reach out of his fate.

The house is like a child's drawing. A deputizing childishness that grew because someone—much too soon—gave up his mission to be a child. Open the door, step in! In here there's unrest in the ceiling and peace in the walls. Above the bed hangs a painting of a ship with seventeen sails, hissing wave crests, and a wind that the gilt frame can't contain.

It's always so early in here, before the crossroads, before the irrevocable choices. Thank you for this life! Still I miss the alternatives. The sketches, all of them, want to become real.

A ship's engine far away on the water expands the summer-night horizon. Both joy and sorrow swell in the dew's magnifying glass. Without really knowing, we divine; our life has a sister ship, following quite another route. While the sun blazes behind the islands.

· III ·

Satellite Eyes

The ground is rough, no mirror.
Only the coarsest of spirits
can reflect themselves: the Moon
and the Ice Age.

Come closer in the dragon haze!
Heavy clouds, milling streets.
A rustling downpour of souls.
Barrack squares.

Nineteen Hundred and Eighty

His glance flits in jerks across the newsprint.
Feelings come, so icy they're taken for thoughts.
Only in deep hypnosis could he be his other I,
his hidden sister, the woman who joins the hundreds of thousands
screaming "Death to the Shah!"—although he is already dead—
a marching black tent, pious and full of hate.
Jihad! Two who shall never meet take the world in hand.

Black Postcards

1

The diary written full, future unknown.
The cable hums the folk song with no home.
Snowfall on the lead-still sea. Shadows
                wrestle on the Pier.

2

In the middle of life it happens that death comes
to take man's measurements. The visit
is forgotten and life goes on. But the suit
                is sewn on the quiet.

Fire-Jottings

Throughout the dismal months my life sparkled alive only when I made
        love with you.
As the firefly ignites and fades out, ignites and fades out—in glimpses we
        can trace its flight
in the dark among the olive trees.

Throughout the dismal months the soul lay shrunken, lifeless,
but the body went straight to you.
The night sky bellowed.
Stealthily we milked the cosmos and survived.

Many Steps

The icons are laid in the earth face up
and the earth trod down again
by wheels and shoes, by thousands of steps,
by the heavy steps of ten thousand doubters.

In my dream I stepped down into a luminous underground pool,
a surging litany.
What sharp longing! What idiotic hope!
And over me the tread of millions of doubters.

Postludium

I drag like a grapnel over the world's floor—
everything catches that I don't need.
Tired indignation. Glowing resignation.
The executioners fetch stone. God writes in the sand.

Silent rooms.
The furniture stands in the moonlight, ready to fly.
I walk slowly into myself
through a forest of empty suits of armor.

• IV •

Dream Seminar

Four thousand million on Earth.
They all sleep, they all dream.
Faces throng, and bodies, in each dream—
the dreamt-of people are more numerous
than us. But take no space. . . .
You doze off at the theater perhaps,
in mid-play your eyelids sink.
A fleeting double exposure: the stage
before you outmaneuvered by a dream.
Then no more stage, it's you.
The theater in the honest depths!
The mystery of the overworked director!
Perpetual memorizing of new plays . . .
A bedroom. Night.
The darkened sky is flowing through the room.
The book that someone fell asleep from lies
still open
sprawling wounded at the edge of the bed.
The sleeper's eyes are moving,
they're following the text without letters
in another book—
illuminated, old-fashioned, swift.
A dizzying commedia inscribed
within the eyelids' monastery walls.
A unique copy. Here, this very moment.
In the morning, wiped out.
The mystery of the great waste!
Annihilation. As when suspicious men
in uniforms stop the tourist—
open his camera, unwind the film
and let the daylight kill the pictures:
thus dreams are blackened by the light of day.
Annihilated or just invisible?

There is a kind of out-of-sight dreaming
that never stops. Light for other eyes.
A zone where creeping thoughts learn to walk.
Faces and forms regrouped.
We're moving on a street, among people
in blazing sun.
But just as many—maybe more—
we don't see
are in dark buildings,
high on both sides.
Sometimes one of them comes to the window
and glances down on us.

Codex

Men of footnotes, not headlines. I find myself in the deep corridor
that would have been dark
if my right hand wasn't shining like a torch.
The light falls on something written on the wall
and I see it
as the diver sees the name on the sunken hull shimmering toward him in
     the flowing depths:
ADAM ILEBORGH 1448. Who?
It was he who made the organ spread its clumpy wings and rise—
and it held itself airborne nearly a minute.
An experiment blessed with success!
Written on the wall: MAYONE, DAUTHENDEY, KAMINSKY ... The light
     touches name upon name.
The walls are quite scrawled over.
They're the names of the all-but-extinct artists
the men of footnotes, the unplayed, the half-forgotten, the immortal
     unknown.
For a moment it feels as if they're all whispering their names at once—
whispering added to whispering till a tumbling breaker cascades along
     the corridor

without throwing anyone down.
Though the corridor is no longer a corridor.
Neither a graveyard nor a marketplace but something of both.
A kind of greenhouse, too.
Plenty of oxygen.
Dead men of the footnotes can breathe deeply, they remain in the eco-
       logical system.
But there is much they are spared.
They are spared swallowing the morality of power,
they are spared the black-and-white checkered game where the smell of
       corpses is the only thing that never dies.
They are rehabilitated.
And those who can no longer receive
have not stopped giving.
They rolled out a little of the radiant and melancholy tapestry
and let go again.
Some are anonymous, they are my friends
without my knowing them, they are like those stone people
carved on grave slabs in old churches.
Soft or harsh reliefs in walls we brush against, figures and names
sunk in the stone floors, on the way to extinction.
But those who really want to be struck from the list . . .
They don't stop in the region of footnotes,
they step into the downward career that ends in oblivion and peace.
Total oblivion. It's a kind of exam
taken in silence: to step over the border without anyone noticing. . . .

Carillon

Madame despises her guests because they want to stay at her shabby
  hotel.
I have the corner room, one floor up: a wretched bed, a lightbulb in the
  ceiling.
Heavy drapes where a quarter of a million mites are on the march.

Outside: a pedestrian street
with slow tourists, hurrying schoolchildren, men in working clothes
  who wheel their rattling bikes.
Those who think they make the earth go round and those who think
  they go round helplessly in earth's grip.
A street we all walk, where does it emerge?

The room's only window faces something else: The Wild Market Square,
ground that seethes, a wide trembling surface, at times crowded and at
  times deserted.

What I carry within me is materialized—all terrors, all expectations.
All the inconceivable that will nevertheless happen.

I have low beaches; if death rises six inches I shall be flooded.
I am Maximilian. It's 1488. I'm held prisoner here in Bruges
because my enemies are irresolute—
they are wicked idealists and what they did in horror's backyard I can't
  describe, I can't turn blood into ink.

I am also the man in overalls wheeling his rattling bike down the street.

I am also the person seen, that tourist, the one loitering and pausing,
  loitering and pausing
and letting his gaze wander over the pale moon-tanned faces and surging
  draperies of old paintings.

No one decides where I go, least of all myself, though each step is where
it must be.
Walking around in the fossil wars where all are invulnerable because all
are dead!
The dusty foliage, the walls with their loopholes, the garden paths where
petrified tears crunch under the heels . . .

Unexpectedly, as if I'd stepped on a tripwire, the bell-ringing starts in the
anonymous tower.
Carillon! The sack splits along its seams and the chimes roll out across
Flanders.
Carillon! The cooing iron of the bells, hymn and hit song in one, written
in the air, trembling.
The shaky-handed doctor wrote a prescription that no one can decipher
but his writing will be recognized. . . .

Over meadow and rooftop, harvest and mart,
over quick and dead the carillon rings.
Christ and Antichrist, hard to tell apart!
The bells bear us home at last on their wings.

They have stopped.

I am back in the hotel room: the bed, the light, the drapes. Strange
noises—the cellar is dragging itself up the stairs.

I lie on the bed with my arms outstretched.
I am an anchor that has dug itself down and holds steady
the huge shadow floating up there
the great unknown that I am a part of and which is certainly more impor-
tant than me.

Outside: the walkway, the street where my steps die away and also what
is written, my preface to silence and my inside-out psalm.

Molokai

We stand at the edge and deep down under us glisten the roofs of the
    leper colony.
The climb down we could manage but we'd never make it back up the
    slopes before nightfall.
So we turn back through the forest, walk among trees with long blue
    needles.
It's silent here, like the silence when the hawk nears.
These are woods that forgive everything but forget nothing.
Damien, for love, chose life and obscurity. He received death and fame.
But we see these events from the wrong side: a heap of stones instead of
    the sphinx's face.

FOR THE LIVING AND THE DEAD
FÖR LEVANDE OCH DÖDA

1989

The Forgotten Captain

We have many shadows. I was walking home
in the September night when Y
climbed out of his grave after forty years
and kept me company.

At first he was quite empty, only a name
but his thoughts swam
faster than time ran
and caught up with us.

I put his eyes to my eyes
and saw war's ocean.
The last boat he captained
took shape beneath us.

Ahead and astern the Atlantic convoy crept,
the ships that would survive
and the ships that bore the Mark
(invisible to all)

while sleepless days and nights relieved each other
but never him.
Under his oilskin, his life jacket.
He never came home.

It was an internal weeping that bled him to death
in a Cardiff hospital.
He could at last lie down
and turn into a horizon.

Good-bye, eleven-knot convoys! Good-bye, 1940!
Here ends world history.
The bombers were left hanging.
The heathery moors blossomed.

A photo from early this century shows a beach.
Six Sunday-best boys.
Sailboats in their arms.
What solemn airs!

The boats that became life and death for some of them.
And writing about the dead—
that too is a game, made heavy
with what is to come.

Six Winters

1

In the black hotel a child is asleep.
And outside: the winter night
where the wide-eyed dice roll.

2

An élite of the dead became stone
in Katarina Churchyard
where the wind shakes in its Svalbard armor.

3

One wartime winter when I lay sick
a huge icicle grew outside the window.
Neighbor and harpoon, unexplained memory.

4

Ice hangs down from the roof-edge.
Icicles: the upside-down Gothic.
Abstract cattle, udders of glass.

5

On a sidetrack an empty railway carriage.
Still. Heraldic.
With the journeys in its claws.

6

Tonight snow-haze, moonlight. The moonlight jellyfish itself
is floating before us. Our smiles
on the way home. Bewitched avenue.

The Nightingale in Badelunda

In the green midnight at the nightingale's northern limit. Heavy leaves
hang in trance, the deaf cars race toward the neon line. The nightingale's
voice rises without wavering to the side, it is as penetrating as a cockcrow,
but beautiful and free of vanity. I was in prison and it visited me. I was sick
and it visited me. I didn't notice it then, but I do now. Time streams down
from the sun and the moon and into all the tick-tock-thankful clocks. But
right here there is no time. Only the nightingale's voice, the raw resonant
notes that whet the night sky's gleaming scythe.

Early May Stanzas

A May wood. The invisible removal load,
   my whole life, like a haunting here. Birds in song.
     In the silent pools, midge larvae—
       their dancing furious question marks.

I escape to the same places, and the same words.
   Cool sea breeze. And the ice-dragon licks the back
     of my neck while sunlight blazes.
       The load is burning with chilly flames.

Berceuse

I am a mummy at rest in the blue coffin of the forests, in the perpetual
     roar of engines and rubber and asphalt.

What happened during the day sinks, the homework is heavier than life.

The wheelbarrow rolled forward on its single wheel and I myself traveled
     on my spinning psyche, but now my thoughts have stopped
     spinning and the wheelbarrow has grown wings.

At long last, when space is black, a plane will come. The passengers will
     see the cities beneath them glittering like the gold of the Goths.

Streets in Shanghai

1

The white butterfly in the park is read by many.
I love that cabbage-white as if it were a fluttering corner of truth itself!

At dawn the crowds get our silent planet going with their running.
The park fills with people. To each one there are eight faces polished like
        jade, for every situation, for the avoidance of mistakes.

To each one, also, the invisible face that mirrors "something one doesn't
        talk about."
Something that turns up in tired moments and is acrid like a mouthful
        of adder-brandy with its lingering scaly aftertaste.

The carp in the pond move perpetually, they swim while they sleep, they
        are models for the faithful: always in motion.

2

It's midday. The washing flutters in the grey sea-wind high above the
        cyclists
who come in dense shoals. Mind the labyrinths to left and right!

I'm surrounded by written signs I can't interpret, I'm totally illiterate.
But I've paid what I should and have receipts for everything.
I've accumulated so many illegible receipts.
I'm an old tree with withered leaves that hang on and can't fall to the
        earth.

And a puff of air from the sea makes all those receipts rustle.

3

At dawn the crowds get our silent planet going with their tramping.
We are all aboard the street. It is packed like the deck of a ferry.
Where are we going? Are there enough teacups? We can count ourselves
       lucky getting aboard this street!
It's a thousand years before the birth of claustrophobia.

Behind each one of us hovers a cross that wants to catch up with us,
       overtake us, unite with us.
Something that wants to creep up behind us and cover our eyes and
       whisper, "Guess who!"

We look almost happy out in the sun, while we are bleeding fatally from
       wounds we don't know about.

Deep in Europe

I a dark hull floating between two lock gates
rest in the hotel bed while the city around me wakens.
The silent clamor and the grey light stream in
and raise me slowly to the next level: the morning.

Overheard horizon. They want to say something, the dead.
They smoke but don't eat, they don't breathe but still have their voices.
I'll be hurrying through the streets like one of them.
The blackened cathedral, heavy as a moon, causes ebb and flow.

Leaflet

The silent rage scribbles on the wall inward.
Fruit trees in blossom, the cuckoo calls.
It's spring's narcosis. But the silent rage
paints its slogans backward in the garages.

We see all and nothing, but straight as periscopes
wielded by the underground's shy crew.
It's the war of the minutes. The blazing sun
stands above the hospital, suffering's parking place.

We living nails hammered down in society!
One day we shall loosen from everything.
We shall feel death's air under our wings
and become milder and wilder than we ever were.

The Indoors Is Endless

It's spring 1827, Beethoven
hoists his death mask and sails off.

The grindstones are turning in Europe's windmills.
The wild geese are flying northward.

Here is the north, here is Stockholm
swimming palaces and hovels.

The logs in the royal fireplace
collapse from Attention to At Ease.

Peace prevails, vaccine and potatoes,
but the city wells breathe heavily.

Privy barrels in sedan chairs like pashas
are carried by night over the North Bridge.

The cobblestones make them stagger
mam'selles loafers gentlemen.

Implacably still, the signboard
with the smoking blackamoor.

So many islands, so much rowing
with invisible oars against the current!

The channels open up: April May
and sweet honey-dribbling June.

The heat reaches islands far out.
The village doors are open, except one.

The snake-clock's pointer licks the silence.
The rock slopes glow with geology's patience.

It happened like this, or almost.
It is an obscure family tale

about Erik, broken down by a curse
disabled by a bullet through the soul.

He went to town, met an enemy
and sailed home sick and grey.

Keeps to his bed all summer.
The tools on the wall are in mourning.

He lies awake, hears the woolly flutter
of night moths, his moonlight comrades.

His strength ebbs out, he pushes in vain
against the ironbound tomorrow.

And the God of the depths cries out of the depths,
"Deliver me! Deliver yourself!"

All the surface action turns inward.
He's taken apart, put together.

The wind rises and the wild rosebushes
catch on the fleeing light.

The future opens, he looks into
the self-rotating kaleidoscope

sees indistinct fluttering faces
family faces not yet born.

By mistake his gaze strikes me
as I walk around in Washington

among grandiose houses where only
every second column bears weight.

White buildings in crematorium style
where the dream of the poor turns to ash.

The gentle downward slope gets steeper
and imperceptibly becomes an abyss.

Vermeer

No protected world . . . Just behind the wall the noise begins,
the inn
with laughter and bickering, rows of teeth, tears, the din of bells
and the insane brother-in-law, the death-bringer we all must tremble for.

The big explosion and the tramp of rescue arriving late,
the boats preening themselves on the straits, the money creeping down
   in the wrong man's pocket
demands stacked on demands
gaping red flowerheads sweating premonitions of war.

And through the wall into the clear studio
into the second that's allowed to live for centuries.
Pictures that call themselves *The Music Lesson*
or *Woman in Blue Reading a Letter*—
she's in her eighth month, two hearts kicking inside her.
On the wall behind is a wrinkled map of Terra Incognita.

Breathe calmly . . . An unknown blue material is nailed to the chairs.
The gold studs flew in with incredible speed
and stopped abruptly
as if they had never been other than stillness.

Ears sing, from depth or height.
It's the pressure from the other side of the wall.
It makes each fact float
and steadies the brush.

It hurts to go through walls, it makes you ill
but is necessary.
The world is one. But walls . . .
And the wall is part of yourself—
we know or we don't know but it's true for us all
except for small children. No walls for them.

The clear sky has leaned against the wall.
It's like a prayer to the emptiness.
And the emptiness turns its face to us
and whispers,
"I am not empty, I am open."

Romanesque Arches

Inside the huge Romanesque church the tourists jostled in the half
        darkness.
Vault gaped behind vault, no complete view.
A few candle flames flickered.
An angel with no face embraced me
and whispered through my whole body:
"Don't be ashamed of being human, be proud!
Inside you vault opens behind vault endlessly.
You will never be complete, that's how it's meant to be."
Blind with tears
I was pushed out on the sun-seething piazza
together with Mr. and Mrs. Jones, Mr. Tanaka, and Signora Sabatini,
and inside each of them vault opened behind vault endlessly.

Epigram

The buildings of capital, the hives of the killer bees, honey for the few.
He served there. But in a dark tunnel he unfolded his wings
and flew when no one was looking. He had to live his life again.

Female Portrait, 19th Century

Her voice is stifled in the clothing. Her eyes
follow the gladiator. Then she herself is
in the arena. Is she free? A gilt frame
                            strangles the picture.

Medieval Motif

Beneath our spellbinding play of faces there waits
inevitably the skull, the poker face. While
the sun's unhurriedly rolling past in the sky.
                        And the chess continues.

A barber-scissor-like clipping sound from the copse.
The sun's unhurriedly rolling past in the sky.
The game of chess comes to a standstill, in a draw.
                        In the rainbow's silence.

Air Mail

On the hunt for a mailbox
I took the letter through the city.
In the big forest of stone and concrete
the straying butterfly flickered.

The flying-carpet of the stamp
the staggering lines of the address
plus my own sealed truth
soaring now over the ocean.

The Atlantic's creeping silver.
The cloud banks. The fishing boat
like a spat-out olive-stone.
And the pale scars of the wakes.

Down here work goes slowly.
I ogle the clock often.
The tree-shadows are black ciphers
in the greedy silence.

The truth's there, on the ground
but no one dares to take it.
The truth's there, on the street.
No one makes it his own.

Madrigal

I inherited a dark wood where I seldom go. But a day will come when the dead and the living change places. The wood will be set in motion. We are not without hope. The most serious crimes will remain unsolved in spite of the efforts of many policemen. In the same way there is somewhere in our lives a great unsolved love. I inherited a dark wood, but today I'm walking in the other wood, the light one. All the living creatures that sing, wriggle, wag, and crawl! It's spring and the air is very strong. I have graduated from the university of oblivion and am as empty-handed as the shirt on the clothesline.

Golden Wasp

The blindworm that legless lizard flows along the porch step
calm and majestic as an anaconda, only the size is different.
The sky is covered with clouds but the sun pushes through. Such is the day.

This morning the woman I love drove away the evil spirits.
As when you open the door of a dark shed somewhere in the south
and the light pours in
and the cockroaches scurry into the corners and up the walls
and are gone—you saw them and you didn't see them—
so her nakedness made the demons run.

As if they never existed.
But they'll come back.
With a thousand hands crossing the lines in the old-fashioned telephone
        exchange of the nerves.

It's the fifth of July. The lupines are stretching up as if they wanted to
        catch sight of the sea.
We're in the church of keeping-silence, of piety according to no letter.
As if they didn't exist, the implacable faces of the patriarchs
and the misspelling of God's name in stone.

I saw a true-to-the-letter TV preacher who'd piled up money.
But he was weak now and needed the support of a bodyguard,
who was a well-tailored young man with a smile tight as a muzzle.
A smile stifling a scream.
The scream of a child left alone in a hospital bed when the parents leave.

The divine brushes against a human being and lights a flame
but then draws back.
Why?
The flame attracts the shadows, they fly rustling in and join the flame,
which rises and blackens. And the smoke spreads out black and
        strangling.
At last only the black smoke, at last only the pious executioner.

The pious executioner leans forward
over the market square and the crowd that make a grainy mirror
in which he can see himself.

The greatest fanatic is the greatest doubter. Without knowing it.
He is a pact between two
where the one is a hundred percent visible and the other invisible.
How I hate that expression "a hundred percent."

Those who can never exist anywhere except on their façades
those who are never absentminded
those who never open the wrong door and catch a glimpse of the Uniden-
      tified One.
Walk past them!

It's the fifth of July. The sky is covered with clouds but the sun pushes
      through.
The blindworm flows along the porch step, calm and majestic as an
      anaconda.
The blindworm as if there were no bureaucracy.
The golden wasp as if there were no idolatry.
The lupines as if there were no "hundred percent."

I know the depth where one is both prisoner and ruler, like Persephone.
I often lay in the stiff grass down there
and watched the earth arch over me.
The vault of the earth.
Often—that was half of my life.

But today my gaze has left me.
My blindness has gone away.
The dark bat has left my face and is scissoring around in summer's
      bright space.

THE SAD GONDOLA

SORGEGONDOLEN

1996

Note: From 19 November 1882 until 13 January 1883, Franz Liszt stayed with his daughter Cosima and her husband, Richard Wagner, at the Palazzo Vendramin, on the Grand Canal in Venice. Inspired by the sight of funeral gondolas, and also "under a premonition," Liszt wrote the two piano pieces *La lugubre gondola I* and *II*. Wagner died on 13 February 1883.

April and Silence

Spring lies desolate.
The velvet-dark ditch
crawls by my side
without reflections.

The only thing that shines
is yellow flowers.

I am carried in my shadow
like a violin
in its black case.

The only thing I want to say
glitters out of reach
like the silver
in a pawnbroker's.

National Insecurity

The Undersecretary leans forward and draws an X
and her eardrops dangle like swords of Damocles.

As a mottled butterfly is invisible against the ground
so the demon merges with the opened newspaper.

A helmet worn by no one has taken power.
The mother turtle flees flying under the water.

A Page of the Nightbook

I stepped ashore one May night
in the cool moonshine
where grass and flowers were grey
but the scent green.

I glided up the slope
in the color-blind night
while white stones
signaled to the moon.

A period of time
a few minutes long
fifty-eight years wide.

And behind me
beyond the lead-shimmering waters
was the other shore
and those who ruled.

People with a future
instead of a face.

The Sad Gondola

1

Two old men, father-in-law and son-in-law, Liszt and Wagner, are stay-
          ing by the Grand Canal
together with the restless woman who married King Midas,
the man who transforms everything he touches into Wagner.
The green chill of the sea forces its way up through the palace floors.
Wagner is marked, the well-known Mr. Punch profile is wearier than
          before
the face a white flag.
The gondola is heavy-laden with their lives, two returns and one single.

2

One of the palace windows flies open and the people inside grimace in
          the sudden draft.
Outside on the water the garbage gondola appears, paddled by two one-
          oared bandits.
Liszt has written some chords that are so heavy they should be sent
to the mineralogical institute in Padua for analysis.
Meteorites!
too heavy to rest, they can only sink and sink through the future right down
to the years of the brownshirts.
The gondola is heavy-laden with the crouching stones of the future.

3

Peepholes, opening on 1990.

March 25. Anxiety over Lithuania.
Dreamt that I visited a large hospital.
No staff. Everyone a patient.

In the same dream a newborn girl
who spoke in complete sentences.

4

Beside his son-in-law, who is a man of the age, Liszt is a moth-eaten
       Grand Seigneur.
It's a disguise.
The deep that tries on and rejects different masks has picked out this one
       for him.
The deep that wants to step in, to visit the humans, without showing its
       face.

5

Abbé Liszt is accustomed to carrying his own suitcase through slush
       and sunshine
and when the time comes to die no one will meet him at the station.
A warm breeze of highly gifted brandy carries him off in the middle of
       some task.
He is never free of tasks.
Two thousand letters per year!
The schoolboy writing out the misspelled word a hundred times before
       he can go home.
The gondola is heavy-laden with life, it is simple and black.

6

1990 again.

Dreamt that I drove 200 kilometers for nothing.
Then everything grew large. Sparrows
big as hens sang deafeningly.

Dreamt that I drew piano keys
on the kitchen table. I played on them, silently.
The neighbors came in to listen.

7

The keyboard, which has kept silent through the whole of *Parsifal* (but it
       has listened) is at last allowed to say something.
Sighs . . . sospiri . . .
When Liszt plays this evening he holds down the sea-pedal
so that the green power of the sea rises through the floor and merges
       with the stonework of the building.
Good evening, beautiful deep!
The gondola is heavy-laden with life, it is simple and black.

8

Dreamt that I was to start school but arrived late.
Everyone in the room was wearing a white mask.
Impossible to tell who the teacher was.

Landscape with Suns

The sun emerges around the house,
stands in the middle of the road
and breathes on us
with its red blast.
Innsbrück I must leave you.
But tomorrow
there will be a glowing sun
in the half-dead grey forest
where we have to work and live.

November in the Former DDR

The almighty cyclop's-eye clouded over
and the grass shook itself in the coal dust.

Beaten black and blue by the night's dreams,
we board the train
that stops at every station
and lays eggs.

Almost silent.
The clang of the church bells' buckets
fetching water.
And someone's inexorable cough
scolding everything and everyone.

A stone idol moves its lips:
it's the city.
Ruled by iron-hard misunderstandings
among kiosk attendants butchers
metalworkers naval officers
iron-hard misunderstandings, academics!

How sore my eyes are!
They've been reading by the faint glimmer of the glowworm lamps.

November offers caramels of granite.
Unpredictable!
Like world history
laughing at the wrong place.

But we hear the clang
of the church bells' buckets fetching water
every Wednesday
—is it Wednesday?—
so much for our Sundays!

From July 1990

It was a funeral
and I felt the dead man
was reading my thoughts
better than I could.

The organ was silent, the birds sang.
The grave out in the sunshine.
My friend's voice belonged
on the far side of the minutes.

I drove home seen through
by the glitter of the summer day
by rain and quietness
seen through by the moon.

The Cuckoo

A cuckoo sat hoo-hooing in the birch just north of the house. It was so loud that at first I thought it was an opera singer imitating a cuckoo. I looked at the bird in surprise. Its tail feathers moved up and down to each note like a pump handle. The bird was bouncing on both feet, turning round, and screaming toward every point of the compass. Then it took off, muttering, and flew over the house away to the west. . . . Summer is growing old and everything is flowing into a single melancholy murmur. *Cuculus canorus* will return to the tropics. Its time in Sweden is over. Its time here was not long! In fact the cuckoo is a citizen of Zaire. . . . I am no longer so fond of making journeys. But the journey visits me. Now when I am more and more pushed into a corner, when the annual growth rings multiply, when I need reading glasses. Always there is much more happening than we can bear. There is nothing to be surprised at. These thoughts bear me as faithfully as Susi and Chuma bore Livingstone's embalmed body right through Africa.

Three Stanzas

1

The knight and his lady
turned to stone but happy
on a flying coffin-lid
outside time.

2

Jesus held up a coin
with Tiberius in profile
a profile without love
power in circulation.

3

A dripping sword
wipes out the memories.
On the ground trumpets
and sword belts rust.

Like Being a Child

Like being a child and a sudden insult
is jerked over your head like a sack
through its mesh you catch a glimpse of the sun
and hear the cherry trees humming.

No help in that—the great insult
covers your head your torso your knees
you can move sporadically
but can't look forward to spring.

Glimmering woolly hat, pull it down over your face
stare through the stitches.
On the straits the water rings are crowding soundlessly.
Green leaves are darkening the earth.

Two Cities

Each on its side of a strait, two cities
the one blacked out, occupied by the enemy.
In the other the lamps are burning.
The bright shore hypnotizes the dark one.

I swim out in a trance
on the glittering dark waters.
A dull tuba blast penetrates.
It's a friend's voice, take up your grave and walk.

The Light Streams In

Outside the window, the long beast of spring
the transparent dragon of sunlight
rushes past like an endless
suburban train—we never got a glimpse of its head.

The shoreline villas shuffle sideways
they are proud as crabs.
The sun makes the statues blink.

The raging sea of fire out in space
is transformed to a caress.
The countdown has begun.

Night Journey

Thronging under us. The trains.
Hotel Astoria trembles.
A glass of water at the bedside
shines in the tunnels.

He dreamt he was a prisoner on Svalbard.
The planet turned rumbling.
Glittering eyes walked over the ice fields.
The beauty of miracles existed.

Haiku

The power lines stretched
across the kingdom of frost
north of all music.

•

The white sun's a long-
distance runner against
the blue mountains of death.

•

We have to live with
the small-print grasses and
laughter from the cellar.

•

The sun is low now.
Our shadows are giants.
Soon all will be shadow.

•

The purple orchids.
Oil tankers are gliding past.
The moon's at the full.

•

Medieval keep.
Alien city, cold sphinx,
empty arenas.

•

The leaves whispering:
a wild boar's at the organ.
And the bells pealed out.

•

The night flows westwards
horizon to horizon
all at the moon's speed.

•

The presence of God.
In the tunnel of birdsong
a locked seal opens.

•

Oak trees and the moon.
Light. Silent constellations.
And the cold ocean.

From the Island, 1860

1

One day as she rinsed clothes from the jetty
the chill of the strait rose through her arms
into her life.

Her tears froze into a pair of glasses.
The island raised itself in the grass
and the banner of Baltic herring swayed in the depths.

2

And the swarm of smallpox caught up with him
clustered onto his face.
He lies and stares at the ceiling.

What plying of oars up the silence.
The moment's eternally running stain
the moment's eternally bleeding point.

Silence

Walk past, they are buried . . .
A cloud glides across the sun's disk.

Starvation is a tall building
that moves by night

in the bedroom an elevator shaft opens—
a dark rod pointing to the inner domains.

Flowers in the ditch. Fanfare and silence.
Walk past, they are buried . . .

The table-silver survives in big shoals
deep down where the Atlantic is black.

Midwinter

A blue sheen
radiates from my clothes.
Midwinter.
Jangling tambourines of ice.
I close my eyes.
There is a soundless world
there is a crack
where dead people
are smuggled across the border.

A Sketch from 1844

William Turner's face is weather-brown.
He has set up his easel far out among the breakers.
We follow the silver-green cable down in the depths.

He wades out in the shelving kingdom of death.
A train rolls in. Come closer.
Rain, rain travels over us.

THE GREAT ENIGMA

DEN STORA GÅTAN

2004

Eagle Rock

Behind the vivarium glass
the reptiles
unmoving.

A woman hangs up washing
in the silence.
Death is becalmed.

In the depths of the ground
my soul glides
silent as a comet.

Façades

1

At road's end I see power
and it's like an onion
with overlapping faces
coming loose one by one . . .

2

The theaters are emptied. It's midnight.
Words blaze on the façades.
The enigma of the unanswered letters
sinks through the cold glitter.

November

When the hangman's bored he turns dangerous.
The burning sky rolls up.

Tapping sounds can be heard from cell to cell
and space streams up from the ground-frost.

A few stones shine like full moons.

Snow Is Falling

The funerals keep coming
more and more of them
like the traffic signs
as we approach a city.

Thousands of people gazing
in the land of long shadows.

A bridge builds itself
slowly
straight out in space.

Signatures

I have to step
over the dark threshold.
A hall.
The white document gleams.
With many shadows moving.
Everyone wants to sign it.

Until the light overtook me
and folded up time.

Haiku

1

With hanging gardens,
a lama monastery.
Painted battle scenes.

•

Wall of hopelessness . . .
The doves flutter to and fro.
They have no faces.

•

Thoughts standing still, like
the colored mosaic stones in
the palace courtyard.

•

On the balcony
I stand in a cage of sun-
beams—like a rainbow.

•

Humming in the mist.
A fishing boat far from land
—trophy on the waves.

•

Glittering cities:
song, stories, mathematics—
but with a difference.

2

Stag in blazing sun.
The flies sew, sew, fasten that
shadow to the ground.

3

A chill-to-the-bone
wind flows through the house tonight—
names of the demons.

•

Gaunt tousled pine trees
on the same tragic moorland.
Always and always.

•

Borne by the darkness.
I met an immense shadow
in a pair of eyes.

•

The November sun—
my enormous shadow swims
becomes a mirage.

•

Those milestones, always
on their way somewhere. Listen
—a stock dove calling.

•

Death stoops over me.
I'm a problem in chess. He
has the solution.

4

The sun disappears.
The tugboat looks on with its
face of a bulldog.

•

On a rocky ledge
the crack in the charmed cliff shows.
The dream an iceberg.

•

Working up the slopes
in open sunlight—the goats
that foraged on fire.

5

And blueweed, blueweed
keeps rising from the asphalt.
It's like a beggar.

·

The darkening leaves
in autumn are as precious
as the Dead Sea Scrolls.

6

Sitting on a shelf
in the library of fools
the sermons untouched.

·

Come out of the swamp!
Sheatfish tremble with laughter
when the pine strikes twelve.

·

My happiness swelled
in those Pomeranian
swamps and the frogs sang.

•

He writes, writes, and writes . . .
Glue floated in the canals.
On the Styx, that barge.

•

Go, quiet as a shower
and meet the whispering leaves.
Hear the Kremlin's bell!

7

Perplexing forest
where God lives without money.
The walls were shining.

•

Encroaching shadows . . .
We are astray in the woods
in the mushroom clan.

•

Black-and-white magpie
stubbornly running zigzag
right across the fields.

.

See how I'm sitting
like a punt pulled up on land.
Here I am happy.

.

The avenues trot
in a harness of sunbeams.
Did someone call out?

8

The grass is rising—
his face is a runic stone
raised in memory.

.

Here's a dark picture.
Poverty painted over,
flowers in prison dress.

9

When the hour is here
the blind wind will come to rest
against the façades.

•

I've been in that place—
all over a whitewashed wall
the flies crowd and crowd.

•

Here where the sun burned . . .
a mast holding a black sail
from long long ago.

•

Hold on, nightingale!
Out of the depths it's growing—
we are in disguise.

10

Death leans forward and
writes on the ocean surface.
While the church breathes gold.

•

Something has happened.
The moon filled the room with light.
God knew about it.

•

The roof broke apart
and the dead man can see me
can see me. That face.

•

Hear the swish of rain.
To reach right into it I
whisper a secret.

•

Station-platform scene.
What unpredictable calm—
it's the inner voice.

11

A revelation.
The long-standing apple tree.
The sea is close by.

•

The sea is a wall.
I can hear the gulls screaming—
they're waving at us.

•

God's wind in the back.
The shot that comes soundlessly—
a much-too-long dream.

•

Ash-colored silence.
The blue giant passes by.
Cool breeze from the sea.

•

A wind vast and slow
from the ocean's library.
Here's where I can rest.

•

Birds in human shape.
The apple trees in blossom.
The great enigma.

MEMORIES LOOK AT ME

MINNENA SER MIG

1993

PROSE MEMOIR

Memories

"My life." Thinking these words, I see before me a streak of light. On closer inspection it has the form of a comet. The brightest end, the head, is childhood and growing up. The nucleus, the densest part, is infancy, that first period, in which the most important features of our life are determined. I try to remember, I try to penetrate that density. But it is difficult to move in these concentrated regions, it is dangerous, it feels as if I am coming close to death itself. Further back, the comet thins out—that's the longer part, the tail. It becomes more and more sparse, but also broader. I am now far out in the comet's tail, I am sixty as I write this.

Our earliest experiences are for the most part inaccessible. Retellings, memories of memories, reconstructions based on moods that suddenly flare into life.

My earliest datable memory is a feeling. A feeling of pride. I have just turned three and it has been declared that this is very significant, that I am now big. I'm in bed in a bright room, then clamber down to the floor stunningly aware of the fact that I am becoming a grown-up. I have a doll to whom I gave the most beautiful name I could think of: Karin Spinna. I don't treat her in a motherly fashion. She is more like a comrade or someone I am in love with.

We live in Stockholm, in the Söder area, at Swedenborgsgatan 33 (now called Grindsgatan). Father is still part of the family but is soon to leave. Our ways are quite "modern"—right from the start I use the familiar *du* form with my parents. My mother's parents are close by, just around the corner, in Blekingegatan.

My maternal grandfather, Carl Helmer Westerberg, was born in 1860. He was a ship's pilot and a very good friend of mine, seventy-one years older than myself. Oddly enough, the same difference in age existed between him and his own maternal grandfather, who was born in 1789: the storming of the Bastille, the Anjala mutiny, Mozart writing his Clarinet Quintet. Two equal steps back in time, two long steps, yet not really so very long. We can touch history.

Grandfather's way of speech belonged to the nineteenth century. Many of his expressions would seem surprisingly old-fashioned today. But in his mouth, and to my ear, they felt altogether natural. He was a fairly short man, with a white moustache and a prominent and rather crooked nose—"like a Turk's," as he said. His temperament was lively and he could flare up at any moment. His occasional outbursts were never taken too seriously and they were over as soon as they had begun. He was quite without persistent aggression. Indeed he was so conciliatory that he risked being labeled as soft. He wanted to keep on the best side even of people who might be criticized—in their absence—in the course of ordinary conversation. "But surely you must agree that X is a crook!" "Well, well—that's something I don't really know about...."

After the divorce, Mother and I moved to Folkungagatan 57, a lower-middle-class tenement, where a motley crowd lived in close proximity to one another. My memories of life in that tenement arrange themselves like scenes from a film of the thirties or forties, with the appropriate list of characters. The lovable concierge, her strong laconic husband whom I admired because, among other things, he had been poisoned by gas, which suggested a heroic closeness to dangerous machines.

A steady trickle of comers and goers didn't belong there. The occasional drunk would slowly return to his wits on the stairway. Several times a week beggars would ring. They would stand on the porch mumbling. Mother made sandwiches for them—she gave them slices of bread rather than money.

We lived on the fifth floor. At the top, that is. There were four doors, plus the entry to the attic. On one of them was the name Orke, press photographer. In a way it seemed grand to live beside a press photographer.

Our next-door neighbor was a bachelor, well into middle age, yellowish complexion. He worked at home, running some sort of broker's business by phone. In the course of his calls he often gave vent to hilarious guffaws that burst through the walls into our apartment. Another recurring sound was the pop of corks. Beer bottles did not have metal caps then. Those Dionysiac sounds, the guffaws of laughter and the popping of corks, seemed hardly to belong to the spectrally pale old fellow we sometimes met in the elevator. As the years passed he became suspicious and the bouts of laughter diminished in frequency.

Once, there was an outbreak of violence. I was quite small. A neighbor had been locked out by his wife; he was drunk and furious and she had barricaded herself in. He tried to break down the door and bawled out various threats. I remember him screaming the peculiar sentence: "I don't give a damn if I go to Kungsholmen!" I asked Mother what he meant, about Kungsholmen. She explained that the police headquarters was there. From then on that part of town evoked a sense of something fearful. (This feeling intensified when I visited St. Erik's Hospital and saw the war-wounded from Finland being cared for in the winter of 1939–40.)

Mother left for work early in the morning. She didn't take a tram or bus—throughout her entire adult life she walked from Söder to Östermalm, Östermalm to Söder. She worked in the Hedvig Leonora School and was in charge of the third and fourth grades year after year. She was a devoted teacher, deeply involved with the children. One might imagine it would be hard for her to accept retirement. But it wasn't—she felt greatly relieved.

Since Mother worked we had home-help, a "maid" as she was called, though "child-minder" would have been nearer the truth. She slept in a tiny room that was really part of the kitchen and which was not included in the official apartment-with-two-rooms-and-kitchen designation of our home.

When I was five or six, our maid was called Anna-Lisa and she came from Eslöv, in Skåne, in the south of Sweden. I thought she was very attractive: frizzy blond hair, a turned-up nose, a mild Skåne accent. She was a lovely person and I still feel something special when I pass Eslöv station. But I have never actually stepped off the train at that magic place.

Anna-Lisa was particularly talented at drawing. Disney figures were her specialty. I myself drew almost uninterruptedly throughout those years, in the late 1930s. Grandfather brought home rolls of brown paper of the sort then used in all the grocery shops, and I filled the sheets with illustrated stories. I had, to be sure, taught myself to write at the age of five. But it was too slow a process. My imagination needed some speedier means of expression. I didn't even have enough patience to draw properly. I developed a kind of shorthand sketching method with figures in violent movement: breakneck drama yet no details. Cartoon strips consumed only by myself.

One day in the mid-1930s I disappeared in the middle of Stockholm. Mother and I had been to a school concert. In the crush by the exit I lost my grasp of her hand. I was carried helplessly away by the human current, and since I was so small I could not be discovered. Darkness was falling over Hötorget. I stood at the exit, robbed of all sense of security. There were people around me but they were intent on their own business. There was nothing to hold on to. It was my first experience of death.

After an initial period of panic I began to think. It should be possible to walk home. It was absolutely possible. We had come by bus. I had knelt on the seat as I usually did and looked out of the window. Drottninggatan had flowed past. What I had to do now, simply, was to walk back the same way, bus stop by bus stop.

I went in the right direction. Of that long walk I have a clear memory of only one part—of reaching Norrbro and seeing the water under the bridge. The traffic here was heavy and I didn't dare set off across the street. I turned to a man who was standing beside me and said: "There's a lot of traffic here." He took me by the hand and led me across.

But then he let go of me. I don't know why this man and all the other unknown adults thought it was quite alright for a little boy to wander by himself through Stockholm on a dark evening. But that's how it was. The remainder of the journey—through Gamla Stan, the old town, over Slussen and into Söder—must have been complicated. Perhaps I homed in on my destination with the help of the same mysterious compass that dogs and carrier pigeons have in them—no matter where they are released they always find their way home. I remember nothing of this part of my journey. Well, yes, I do—I remember how my self-confidence grew and grew, so that when I did at last arrive home I was euphoric. Grandfather met me. My devastated mother was sitting in the police station following the progress of their search for me. Grandfather's firm nerves didn't fail him; he received me quite naturally. He was relieved of course, but didn't make a fuss. It all felt secure and natural.

Museums

As a child I was attracted to museums. First, the Natural History Museum. What a building! Gigantic, Babylonian, inexhaustible! On the ground floor, hall after hall of stuffed mammals and birds thronged in the dust. And the arches, smelling of bones, where the whales hung from the roof. Then one floor up: the fossils, the invertebrates . . .

I was taken to the Natural History Museum when I was only about five years old. At the entrance, two elephant skeletons met the visitor. They were the two guardians of the gateway to the miraculous. They made an overwhelming impression on me and I drew them in a big sketchbook.

After a time, those visits to the Natural History Museum stopped. I started to go through a phase of being quite terrified of skeletons. The worst was the bony figure depicted at the end of the article on "Man" in the *Nordic Family Lexicon*. But my fear was aroused by skeletons in general, including the elephant skeletons at the entrance to the museum. I became frightened even of my own drawing of them and couldn't bring myself to open the sketchbook.

My interest turned to the Railway Museum. Nowadays it occupies spacious premises just outside the town of Gävle, but back then the entire museum was squeezed into a part of the district of Klara right in the center of Stockholm. Twice a week Grandfather and I made our way down from Söder and visited the museum. Grandfather himself must have been enthralled by the model trains, otherwise he would hardly have endured so many visits. When we decided to make a day of it we would finish up in Stockholm Central Station, which was nearby, and watch the trains come steaming in, lifesized.

The museum staff noticed the zeal of the young boy, and on one occasion I was taken into the museum office and allowed to write my name (with a back-to-front S) in a visitors' book. I wanted to be a railway engineer. I was, however, more interested in steam engines than in electric ones. In other words, I was more romantic than technical.

Some time later, as a schoolboy, I returned to the Natural History Museum. I was now an amateur zoologist, solemn, like a little professor. I sat bent over books about insects and fish.

I had started my own collections. They were kept at home in a cupboard. But inside my skull grew an immense museum and a kind of interplay developed between this imaginary one and the very real one that I visited.

I visited the Natural History Museum more or less every second Sunday. I took the tram to Roslagstull and walked the rest of the way. The road was always a little longer than I had imagined. I remember those foot marches very clearly: it was always windy, my nose ran, my eyes filled with tears. I don't remember the journeys in the opposite direction. It's as if I never went home, only out to the museum, a sniffling, tearful, hopeful expedition toward a giant Babylonian building.

Finally arriving, I would be greeted by the elephant skeletons. I often went directly to the "old" part, the section with animals that had been stuffed back in the eighteenth century, some of them rather clumsily prepared, with swollen heads. Yet there was a special magic here. Big artificial landscapes with elegantly designed and positioned animal models failed to catch my interest—they were make-believe, something for children. No, it had to be quite clear that this was not a matter of living animals. They were stuffed, they stood there in the service of science. The scientific method I was closest to was the Linnean: discover, collect, examine.

I would work slowly through the museum. Long pauses among the whales and in the paleontology rooms. And then what detained me most: the invertebrates.

I never had any contact with other visitors. In fact, I don't remember other visitors being there at all. Other museums I occasionally visited— the National Maritime Museum, the National Museum of Ethnography, the Museum of Technology—were always crowded. But the Natural History Museum seemed to stay open only for me.

One day, however, I did encounter someone—no, not a visitor, he was a professor of some sort. We met among the invertebrates—he suddenly materialized between the display cases, and was almost as small in stature as I was. He spoke half to himself. At once we were involved in a discussion of molluscs. He was so absentminded or so unprejudiced that he treated me like an adult. One of those guardian angels who appeared now and then in my childhood and touched me with its wings.

Our conversation resulted in my being allowed into a section of the museum not open to the public. I was given much good advice on the preparation of small animals, and was equipped with little glass tubes that seemed to me truly professional.

I collected insects, above all beetles, from the age of eleven until I turned fifteen. Then other competing interests, mostly artistic, forced their attentions on me. How melancholy it felt that entomology must give way! I convinced myself that this was only a temporary adjustment. In fifty years or so I would resume my collecting.

My collecting would begin in the spring and then flourished of course in the summer, out on the island of Runmarö. In the summerhouse, where we had little enough space to move around, I kept jam jars with dead insects and a display board for butterflies. And lingering everywhere: the smell of ethyl acetate, a smell I carried with me since I always had a tin of this insect killer in my pocket.

It would no doubt have been more daring to use potassium cyanide as the handbook recommended. Fortunately, this substance was not within my reach, so I never had to test my courage by choosing whether or not to use it.

Many were involved in the insect hunt. The neighborhood children learned to sound the alarm when they saw an insect that could be of interest. "Here's one!" echoed among the houses, and I would come rushing along with my butterfly net.

I went on endless expeditions. A life in the open air without the slightest thought of thereby improving my health. I had no aesthetic opinions on my booty, of course—this was, after all, Science—but I unknowingly absorbed many experiences of natural beauty. I moved in the great mystery. I learned that the ground was alive, that there was an infinite world of creeping and flying things living their own rich life without paying the least regard to us.

I caught a fraction of a fraction of that world and pinned it down in my boxes, which I still have. A hidden mini-museum of which I am seldom conscious. But they're sitting there, those insects. As if biding their time.

Primary School

I began in Katarina Norra Primary School and my teacher was Miss R., a tidy spinster who changed her clothes every day. When school ended each Saturday, each child was given a caramel, but otherwise she was strict. She was generous when it came to pulling hair and delivering blows, although she never hit me. I was the son of a teacher.

The first term, my chief task was to sit still at my desk. I could already write and count. I was allowed to sit and cut out shapes in colored paper, but what the shapes were I can't remember.

I have a feeling that the atmosphere was fairly good throughout my first year but that it chilled somewhat as time passed. Any disturbance to good order, any hitches or snags, made Miss R. lose her temper. We were not allowed to be restless or loud. We were not to whine. We were not to experience unexpected difficulties in learning something. Above all, we were not to do anything unexpected. Any little child who wet himself or herself in shame and fear could not hope for mercy.

As I said, being the son of a teacher saved me from blows. But I could feel the oppressive atmosphere generated by all those threats and reproaches. The head teacher was always in the background—hawk-nosed and dangerous. The very worst prospect was to be sent to a reform school, something which would be mentioned on special occasions. I never felt this as a threat to me personally, but the very idea caused a disagreeable sensation.

I could well imagine what a reformatory was like, the more so since I'd heard the name of one—Skrubba ("Scrub"), a name suggesting rasps and planes. I took it as self-evident that the inmates were subjected to daily torture. The world view that I had acquired allowed for the existence of special institutions where adults tortured children—perhaps to death—for having been noisy. A dreadful outlook. But so be it. If we were noisy, then . . .

When a boy from our school was taken to a reformatory and then returned after a year, I regarded him as someone who had risen from the dead.

A more realistic threat was evacuation. During the first years of the war, plans were made for the evacuation of all schoolchildren from the bigger cities. Mother wrote the name TRANSTRÖMER with marking ink on our sheets, and so on. The question was whether I would be evacuated with mother and her school class or with my own class from Katarina Norra, i.e. deported with Miss R. I suspected the latter.

I escaped evacuation. Life at school went on. I spent all my time in school longing for the day to come to an end so that I could throw myself into what really interested me: Africa, the underwater world, the Middle Ages, etc. The only thing that really caught my attention in school was the wall charts. I was a devotee of wall charts. My greatest happiness was to accompany Miss R. to the storeroom to fetch some worn cardboard chart. While doing so I would peep at the other ones hanging inside. I tried to make some at home, as best I could.

One important difference between my life and that of my classmates was that I could not produce any father. The majority of my peers came from working-class families for whom divorce was clearly very rare. I would never admit that there was anything peculiar about my domestic situation. Not even to myself. No, of course I had a father, even if I saw him only once a year (usually on Christmas Eve). And I kept track of him—at one point during the war, for example, he was on a torpedo boat and sent me an amusing letter. I would have liked to have shared this letter in class but the opportunity never came up.

I remember a moment of panic. I had been absent for a couple of days, and when I came back a classmate told me that the teacher —not Miss R. but a substitute—had said to the class that they must not tease me on account of the fact that I had no father. In other words, they felt sorry for me. I panicked: I was obviously abnormal. I tried to talk it all away, my face bright red.

I was acutely aware of the danger of being regarded as an outsider because at heart I suspected I was one. I was absorbed in interests that no normal boy had. I joined a drawing class, voluntarily, and sketched underwater scenes: fish, sea urchins, crabs, shells. Teacher remarked out loud that my drawings were very "special" and my panic returned. There was a kind of insensitive adult who always wanted to point me out as somehow odd. My classmates were much more tolerant. I was neither popular nor bullied.

Hasse, a big darkish boy who was five times stronger than I was, had a habit of wrestling with me every break during our first year at school. In the beginning I resisted violently, but that got me nowhere for he just threw me to the ground and triumphed over me. At last I thought up a way of disappointing him: total relaxation. When he approached me I pretended that my Real Self had flown away leaving only a corpse behind, a lifeless rag that he could press to the ground as he wished. He soon lost interest.

I wonder what this method of turning myself into a lifeless rag has meant for me later on in life. The art of being ridden roughshod over while yet maintaining one's self-respect. Have I resorted to the trick too often? Sometimes it works, sometimes not.

The War

It was the spring of 1940. I was a skinny nine-year-old stooped over the newspaper, intent on the war map where black arrows indicated the advance of the German tank divisions. Those arrows penetrated France and for us, Hitler's enemies, they lived as parasites in our bodies. I really counted myself as one of Hitler's enemies. My political engagement has never been so wholehearted!

To write of the political engagement of a nine-year-old no doubt invites derision, but this was hardly a question of politics in the proper sense of the word. It meant simply that I took part in the war. I hadn't the slightest conception of matters such as social problems, classes, trade unions, the economy, the distribution of resources, the rival claims of socialism and capitalism. A "Communist" was someone who supported Russia. "Right wing" was a shady term since those at that end of the political spectrum often had German leanings. And were understood to be rich. Yet what did it really mean to be rich? On a few occasions we were invited for a meal with a family who were described as rich. They lived in Äppelviken and the master of the house was a wholesale dealer. A large villa, servants in black and white. I noticed that the boy in the family—he was my age—had an incredibly big toy car, a fire engine, highly desirable. How did one get hold of such a thing? I had a momentary glimpse of the idea that the family belonged to a different social class, one in which people could afford unusually large toy cars. This is still an isolated and not very important memory.

Another memory: during a visit to a classmate's home, I was surprised there was no toilet, only a dry closet out in the backyard, like the kind we had in the country. We would pee into a discarded saucepan which my friend's mother would swill down the kitchen sink. It was picturesque detail. On the whole it didn't occur to me that the family lacked this or that. And the villa in Äppelviken did not strike me as remarkable. I was far short of the capacity that many seem to have acquired, even in their early years, of grasping the class status and economic level of a given environment merely at a glance. Many children seemed able to do so, not I.

My "political" instincts were directed entirely at the war and Nazism. I believed one was either a Nazi or an anti-Nazi. I had no understanding of that lukewarm attitude, that opportunistic wait-and-see stance which was widespread in Sweden. I interpreted this either as support for the Allies or as covert Nazism. When I realized some person I liked was really "pro-German," I immediately felt a terrible tightening over my breast. Everything was ruined. There could never be any kind of fellow feeling between us.

From those close to me I expected unequivocal support. One evening when we were on a visit to Uncle Elof and Aunt Agda, the news inspired my generally taciturn uncle to comment that "the English are successfully retreating . . ." He said this with slight regret mixed with an ironic undertone (on the whole irony was foreign to him) and I suddenly felt that terrible tightening. The Allied version of history was never questioned. I stared grimly up at the roof light for consolation. It had the shape of a British steel helmet: like a soup plate.

On Sundays we often had dinner in Enskede with my other uncle and aunt on Mother's side; they provided a sort of surrogate family for Mother after the divorce. It was part of their ritual to turn on the BBC's Swedish radio broadcast. I shall never forget the program's opening flourish: first the victory signal and then the signature tune, which was alleged to be Purcell's *Trumpet Voluntary* but which in fact was a rather puffed-up arrangement of a harpsichord piece by Jeremiah Clarke. The announcer's calm voice, with a shade of an accent, spoke directly to me from a world of friendly heroes who saw to it that it was business as usual even if bombs were raining down.

When we were on the suburban train on the way to Enskede I always wanted Mother—who hated attracting attention—to unfold the propaganda paper *News from Great Britain,* and thus silently make public our stance. She did nearly everything for me, including that.

I seldom met Father during the war. But one day he popped up and took me to a party with his journalist friends. The glasses were standing ready, there were voices and laughter, and the cigarette smoke was dense. I was led around, being introduced and answering questions. The atmosphere was relaxed and tolerant and I could do what I wanted. I withdrew by myself and sidled along the bookshelves of this strange house.

I came across a newly published book called *The Martyrdom of Poland.* Documentary. I settled on the floor and read it from cover to cover while the voices filled the air. That terrible book—which I have never seen again—contained what I feared, or perhaps what I hoped for. The Nazis were as inhuman as I had imagined—no, they were worse! I read fascinated and disturbed, and at the same time a feeling of triumph emerged:

I'd been right! It was all in the book, detailed proof! Just wait! One day everything will be revealed; one day all of you who have doubted will have the truth thrown in your faces. Just wait! And that, in the event, is what happened.

Libraries

Medborgarhuset (The Citizens' House) was built around 1940. A big four-square block in the middle of Söder, but also a bright and promising edifice, modern, "functional." It was only five minutes from where we lived.

It contained, among other things, a public swimming pool and a branch of the city library. The children's section was, by obvious natural necessity, my allotted sphere, and in the beginning had enough books for my consumption. The most important was Brehm's *Lives of the Animals*.

I slipped into the library nearly every day. But this was not an entirely trouble-free process. It sometimes happened that I tried to borrow books that the library ladies did not consider suitable for my age. One was Knut Holmboe's violent documentary *The Desert Is Burning*.

"Who is to have this book?"

"I am . . ."

"Oh no . . ."

"I . . ."

"You can tell your father he can come and borrow it himself."

It was even worse when I tried to get into the adult section. I needed a book that was definitely not in the children's section. I was stopped at the entrance.

"How old are you?"

"Eleven."

"You can't borrow books here. You can come back in a few years."

"Yes, but the book I want is only in here."

"What book?"

"*The Animals of Scandinavia: A History of Their Migration.*" And I added, "by Ekman," in hollow tones, feeling the game was lost. It was. Out of the question. I blushed, I was furious. I would never forgive her!

In the meantime my uncle of few words—Uncle Elof—intervened. He gave me his card to the adult section and we maintained the fiction that I was collecting books for him. I could now get in where I wanted.

The adult section shared a wall with the pool. At the entrance one felt the fumes from within, the chlorine smell drifted through the ventilation system and the echoing voices could be heard as from a distance. Swimming pools and suchlike always have strange acoustics. The temple of health and the temple of books were neighbors—a good idea. I was a faithful visitor to the Medborgarhus branch of the city library for many years. I regarded it as clearly superior to the central library up on Sveavägen— where the atmosphere was heavier and the air was still, no fumes of chlorine, no echoing voices. The books themselves had a different smell there; it gave me headaches.

Once given free rein of the library I devoted my attention mostly to nonfiction. I left literature to its fate. Likewise the shelves marked Economics and Social Problems. History, though, was interesting. Medicine scared me.

But it was Geography that was my favorite corner. I was a special devotee of the Africa shelves, which were extensive. I can recall titles like *Mount Elgon, A Market-Boy in Africa, Desert Sketches* . . . I wonder if any of those books still fill the shelves.

Someone called Albert Schweitzer had written a book enticingly called *Between Water and Primeval Forest*. It consisted mostly of speculations about life. But Schweitzer himself stayed put in his mission and didn't move; he wasn't a proper explorer. Not like, for instance, Gösta Moberg, who covered endless miles (why?) in alluring, unknown regions, such as Niger or Chad, lands about which there was scant information in the library. Kenya and Tanganyika, however, were favored on account of their Swedish settlements. Tourists who sailed up the Nile to the Sudd area and then turned north again—they wrote books. But not those who ventured into the arid zones of the Sudan, nor those who made their way into Kordofan or Darfur. The Portuguese colonies of Angola and Mozambique, which looked so big on the map, were also unknown and neglected areas on the Africa shelves, making them even more attractive.

I read a lot of books while in the library—I didn't want to take home too many books of the same kind, or the same book several times in succession. I felt I would be criticized by the library staff and that was something to be avoided at all costs.

One summer—I don't remember which one—I lived through an elaborate and persistent daydream about Africa. I was on the island of Runmarö, a long way from the library. I withdrew into a fantasy and was leading an expedition straight through central Africa. I trudged on through the woods of Runmarö and kept track of roughly how far I'd gone with a dotted line on a big map of Africa, a map of the whole continent that I had drawn. If I worked out, for instance, that in the course of a week I had walked 120 kilometers on Runmarö, I marked 120 kilometers on the map. Not very far.

At first I'd thought of starting the expedition on the east coast, more or less where Stanley had begun. But that would have left too great a distance to traverse before I could reach the most interesting parts. I changed my mind and imagined that I traveled as far as Albert Nyansa by car. And this was where the expedition proper started, on foot. I would then have at least a reasonable chance of putting most of the Ituri Forest behind me before summer ended.

It was a nineteenth-century expedition, with bearers, etc. I was half aware, though, that this was now an obsolete way of traveling. Africa had changed. There was war in British Somaliland; it was in the news. Tanks were in action. Indeed, it was the first area where the Allies could claim an advance—I took due note of this, of course—and Abyssinia was the first country to be liberated from the Axis powers.

When my Africa dream returned several years later, it became modernized and was now almost realistic. I was thinking of becoming an entomologist and collecting insects in Africa, discovering new species instead of new deserts.

Grammar School

Only a couple of my classmates from primary school progressed to secondary school (*realskola*). And no one apart from myself applied to Södra Latin Grammar School.

There was an entrance exam I had to pass. My sole memory of this is spelling the word *särskilt* (especially) wrong: I gave it two *l*s. From then on the word had a disturbing effect on me which persisted far into the 1960s.

I have a distinct memory of my first day at Södra Latin in the autumn of 1942. It is as follows: I find myself surrounded by a number of unfamiliar eleven-year-old boys. I have butterflies in my stomach; I'm uncertain and alone. But some of the others seem to know each other well—these are the pupils from Maria Preparatory. I look and look for a face from Katarina Norra. My mood consists of equal parts gloomy unease and hopeful expectation.

Our names are called out and we are divided into three classes. I am assigned to Class 15B and told to follow Dr. Mohlin, who is to be our teacher. He's one of the oldest teachers; his subject is German. He is small, with a sort of catlike authority, and moves swiftly and quietly; he has bristly, reluctantly greying hair, and a bald wedge above each temple. From someone nearby who seems to know him, I catch an assessment of him: Målle—as he is called —is "strict but fair." Ominous.

From the first moment it was clear that grammar school was something quite different from primary school. Södra Latin was thoroughly masculine, the school was as single-sexed as a monastery or barracks. It was not until several years later that a couple of women were smuggled onto the staff.

Each morning we all assembled in the school hall, sang hymns, and listened to a sermon delivered by one of the religious studies teachers. Then we marched off to our respective classrooms. The collective atmosphere of Södra Latin was immortalized by Ingmar Bergman in his film *Hets.** (It was shot in the school and those of us who were pupils appeared as extras in several scenes of the film.)

We were all supplied with a school manual that included, among other items, "Directives as to order and discipline, in accordance with the school's statutes":

> The pupils shall attend instruction at the determined times, neatly and decently attired and in possession of the necessary textbooks. They shall observe good order and proper conduct and shall follow the instruction with due attention. The pupils shall likewise attend morning devotions and there deport themselves quietly and attentively. . . .

---

* In Britain the film was called *Frenzy,* and in the USA, *Torment.*

> Pupils shall give due respect and obedience to the staff of the institu-
> tion and shall accept with compliance their commands, corrections,
> and chastisements. . . .

Södra Latin occupied the highest site on Söder, and its playground
formed a plateau above most of the district's rooftops. The bricks of the
school building could be seen from far away. The route to this castle of
sighs was one I generally completed at a half-run. I hurried along by the
long piles of wood—a sign of the crisis years—in front of "Björns Träd-
gård," made my way up Götgatan—past Hansson and Bruce's bookshop
—swung to the left into Höbergsgatan where, every winter morning, a
horse stood chewing straw from a nosebag. It was a brewery horse, a big
steaming Ardenne. For a moment I found myself in its reeking shadow. I
still have a vivid memory of this patient beast, its smell in the cold and
damp. A smell that was at once suffocating and comforting.

I would rush into the playground just as the bells began to summon us
to morning service. I was hardly ever late, for everything between the
hours of eight and nine in the morning was well-timed. The spring was
firm and tense as the school day began.

The end of the day at school was, of course, more relaxed, less regu-
lated. Sometimes I went home with Palle. He was my closest friend during
my first year at Södra Latin. We had quite a lot in common: his father, a
sailor, was absent for long periods, and he was the only child of a good-
natured mother who seemed pleased to see me. Palle had developed
many of the characteristics of a single child, as I had, and he lived for his
interests. He was above all a collector. Of what? Anything. Beer labels,
matchboxes, swords, flint axes, stamps, postcards, shells, ethnographic
oddities, and bones.

In his home, which was crammed full of his booty, we would duel with
the swords. Together we carried out excavations at a secret spot on Rid-
darholmen and managed to retrieve bits of skeleton, which my dentist
identified as "parts of a human being."

Having Palle as a friend was an enriching experience, but we gradually
drifted apart. Further on in school Palle was absent for long stretches be-
cause of illness. When he was transferred to another class we lost touch.
My old friend was very far away. In fact, he was marked by death. He ap-
peared at school now only occasionally, pale and serious, with one leg
amputated. When he died I found it impossible to accept. I developed a

bad conscience but refused to recognize it. I felt as if I was supposed to suppress the memory of all the fun we'd had.

I feel I'm the same age as Palle, who died forty-five years ago without having grown up. But my old teachers, the "oldies" as they were collectively termed, remain old in my memory in spite of the fact that the older among them were about the same age as I am now as I write this. We always feel younger than we are. I carry inside myself my earlier faces, as a tree contains its rings. The sum of them is "me." The mirror sees only my latest face, while I know all my previous ones.

The teachers who stand out in my memory are, of course, those who generated tension or excitement, those who were vivid, colorful, original. They were not in the majority but there were a fair number of them. We were able to sense something tragic about some of them. A critical situation that could be described thus: "I know I can't be loved by those enviable turnipheads in front of me. I know I can't be loved, but at least I can make sure I won't be forgotten!"

The classroom was a theater. The leading player, the teacher, performed on the stage, subjected to merciless scrutiny. The pupils were the audience and sometimes—one at a time—they would act a part as well.

We had to be on our guard, unfailingly. I had to get used to the recurring outbursts of aggression. Miss R. had laid a good foundation—she had been strict and heavy-handed. Yet not really theatrical. At home there was nothing like this for me to learn—no scenes, no rows, no bellowing father figure. Mother was spontaneous but undramatic. Giving vent to anger was childish. I had often been furious as a child but now I was a reasonably balanced youngster. My ideals were English—a stiff upper lip and so on. Outbursts of rage belonged to the Axis Powers.

At school there were choleric prima donnas who could devote most of a lesson to building up a tower of hysterical indignation with the sole purpose of then emptying their vessels of wrath.

My class teacher, Målle, was hardly a prima donna. But he was the victim of a periodic and irresistible fury. Målle was really a charming person and a good teacher in his more harmonious periods. But, unhappily, what I remember best is his fury. Possibly the more violent outbursts did not come more often than three or four times a month. But it was upon those occasions that his great authority undoubtedly rested.

In the course of such lessons the thunder rolled back and forth across the landscape. That lightning would strike was clear to everyone, but no one could predict where. Målle did not victimize certain pupils. He was "strict but fair." Anyone might be struck by lightning.

One day lightning struck me. We were told to open our German grammars. I couldn't find mine. Was it in my schoolbag? Forgotten at home? I was lost. I couldn't find it.

"Stand up!"

I saw Målle dance down from his desk and close in on me. It was like being out in a field watching a bull approach.

The cuffs rained on me. I staggered this way and that. The next moment Målle was back sitting at his desk, frothing with rage, writing out a note for home. It was worded rather vaguely, accusing me of having been "careless during a lesson" or something.

Many of the teachers hoped those written notes home would lead to interrogations and the infliction of further punishments at the hands of parents.

Not so with me. Mother listened to my story, took the note, and signed it. She then noticed that I had blue marks on my face, caused by the ringed hand of the pedagogue. Her reaction was unexpectedly strong. She said she would contact the school, perhaps phone the headmaster.

I protested. She couldn't do that! Everything had turned out OK. But now "scandal" threatened. I would be called a "mama's boy" and then persecuted forever, not just by Målle but by the entire staff.

She dropped the idea of course. And throughout my school days I made a point of keeping the two worlds—school and home—apart. If the two worlds were to seep into each other, then home would feel polluted. I would no longer have any proper refuge. Even today I find something disagreeable in the phrase "cooperation between home and school." I can also see that this holding apart of the separate worlds that I practiced gave rise in due course to a more deliberately maintained distinction between private life and society. (This has nothing to do with political inclinations, whether to the left or to the right.) What we live through in school is projected as an image of society. My total experience of school was mixed, with more darkness than light—just as my image of society has become. (Although we could well ask what we mean by "society.")

Contact between teacher and pupil was intensely personal, and important personal characteristics were magnified in the classroom atmosphere as the result of the many tense situations. Personal, yes, but not in the slightest private. We knew virtually nothing about the private life of our teachers although most of them lived in the streets around the school. There were, naturally, rumors—like Målle having been a featherweight boxer in his youth—but they were feebly supported by proper evidence and we scarcely gave them credit. We had trustworthy information about two of the most discreet younger teachers, men who never inspired any drama. One of them was poor and eked out his salary by playing the piano at a restaurant in the evening. He was seen. The other was a chess champion. He was in the newspaper.

One day in autumn Målle came into a lesson with a *Russula aerugina* in his hand. He set the mushroom on his desk. It was both liberating and shocking to have caught a glimpse of his private life! We now knew Målle gathered mushrooms.

None of the teachers expressed political opinions. But at that time there were of course unprecedented tensions in the staff room. The Second World War was being fought here, too. Many of the teachers were committed Nazis. As late as 1944 one of them, it was said, exclaimed in the staff room, "If Hitler falls, then *I* shall fall!" He didn't fall, however. I had him in German later. He recovered so well that he was able to welcome Hesse's Nobel Prize in 1946 with triumphant bellowing.

I was a worthy pupil but not one of the best. Biology ought to have been my favorite subject, but for most of my secondary schooling I had a peculiar biology teacher. At some point in the past he had hopelessly blotted his copybook; he was warned and was now like a quenched volcano. My best subjects were geography and history. An assistant teacher called Brännman taught these classes. Ruddy and energetic, Brännman was a youngish man whose straight blond hair had a tendency to stand on end when he got angry, which happened quite often. He had plenty of goodwill and I liked him. The essays I wrote were always on geographical or historical subjects. They were long. Regarding this, I heard a story much later from another Södra Latin pupil, Bo Grandien.* Bo became a close friend of mine in the later years of school but what he told me related to an earlier year when we didn't know each other.

He said the first time he heard my name mentioned was as he passed

---

* Poet and journalist (b. 1932).

some of my classmates during a break. They had just been given back their essays and were dissatisfied with their grades. Bo heard the indignant remark: "We can't *all* write as fast as Tranan, can we?"*

Bo decided that "Tranan" was a detestable character who ought to be avoided. To me, this story is in a way comforting. Nowadays, well-known for deficient productivity, I was then clearly noted as a prolific scribbler, someone who sinned through excessive productivity, a literal Stakhanov.

Exorcism

During the winter when I was fifteen I was afflicted by a severe form of anxiety. I was trapped by a searchlight that radiated not light but darkness. I was caught each afternoon as twilight fell and not released from its terrible grip until the next day dawned. I slept very little; I sat up in bed, usually with a thick book before me. I read several thick books during this time but I can't say I really read them, for they left no trace in my memory. The books were a pretext for leaving the light on.

It began in late autumn. One evening I'd gone to the cinema and seen *Squandered Days,* a film about an alcoholic. It ends with him in a state of delirium—a harrowing sequence that today I would perhaps find rather childish. But not then.

As I lay down to sleep I reran the film in my mind's eye, as one does after being at the cinema.

Suddenly the atmosphere in the room was tense with dread. Something took total possession of me. Suddenly my body started shaking, especially my legs. I was a clockwork toy that had been wound up and now rattled and jumped helplessly. The cramps were quite beyond the control of my will—I had never experienced anything like this. I screamed for help and Mother appeared. Gradually the cramps ebbed away. And did not return. But my dread intensified and from dusk to dawn would not leave me alone. The feeling that dominated my nights was the terror Fritz Lang nearly captured in certain scenes of *The Testament of Dr. Mabuse,* especially the opening scene: a factory where someone hides while the ma-

---

* "Tranan": the crane (the bird).

chines and room vibrate. I recognized myself in this immediately, although my nights were quieter.

The most important element in my existence was *illness*. The world was a vast hospital. I saw before me human beings deformed in body and in soul. The light burned and tried to hold back the terrible faces but sometimes I would doze off, my eyelids would close, and the terrible faces would suddenly close in on me.

It all happened in silence, yet within the silence voices were endlessly busy. The wallpaper pattern made faces. Now and then the silence would be broken by a ticking in the walls. Produced by what? By whom? By me? The walls crackled because my sick thoughts wanted them to. So much the worse . . . Was I insane? Almost.

I was afraid of drifting into madness but in general I did not feel threatened by any kind of illness—it was scarcely a case of hypochondria—but it was rather the total power of illness that aroused terror. As in a film where an innocuous apartment interior changes its character entirely when ominous music is heard, I now experienced the outer world quite differently because it included my awareness of the domination wielded by sickness. A few years previously I had wanted to be an explorer. Now I had pushed my way into an unknown country where I had never wanted to be. I had discovered an evil power. Or rather, the evil power had discovered me.

I read recently about some teenagers who lost all their joy in living because they became obsessed with the idea that AIDS had taken over the world. They would have understood me.

Mother had witnessed the cramps I suffered that evening in late autumn as my crisis began. But then she could only be an outsider. Everyone had to be excluded; what was going on was just too terrible to be discussed. I was surrounded by ghosts. I myself was a ghost. A ghost who walked to school every morning and sat through the lessons without revealing its secret. School had become a breathing space, my dread wasn't the same there. It was my private life that was haunted. Everything was upside down.

At that time I was skeptical of all forms of religion and I certainly said no prayers. If the crisis had arisen a few years later I would have been able to experience it as a revelation, something that would rouse me, like Siddhartha's four encounters (with an old person, with a sick person, with a corpse, and with a begging monk). I would have managed to feel a little more sympathy for, and a little less dread of, the deformed and the sick who invaded my nocturnal consciousness. But back then, caught in my dread, religiously colored explanations were not available to me. No prayers, but attempts at exorcism by way of music. I began to hammer at the piano in earnest.

And all the time I was growing. At the beginning of the autumn term I was one of the smallest in the class, but by its end I was one of the tallest. As if the dread I lived in were a kind of fertilizer helping the plant shoot up.

Winter moved toward its end and the days lengthened. Now, miraculously, the darkness in my own life withdrew. It happened gradually and I was slow in fully realizing what was happening. One spring evening I discovered that all my terrors were now marginal. I sat with some friends philosophizing and smoking cigars. It was time to walk home through the pale spring night and I had no dread at all of terrors waiting for me at home.

Still, it is something I have taken part in. Possibly my most important experience. But it came to an end. I thought it was the Inferno but it was Purgatory.

Latin

In the autumn of 1946 I entered the Latin division of senior secondary school (upper high school). This meant new teachers: instead of Målle, Satan, Slöman (*slö* = dull), and company came characters like Fjalar, Fido, Lillan (the littl'un), Moster (Auntie), and Bocken (The Buck). The last of these was the most important because he was my class teacher and influenced me more than I would have been willing to admit then as our personalities clashed.

A few years before he became my teacher, we had had a moment of dramatic contact. I was late one day and was running along one of the school corridors. Another boy came hurtling in the opposite direction toward me. This was G., who belonged to a parallel class and was well known as a bully. We screeched to a halt, face-to-face, without managing quite to avoid a collision. This sudden braking generated a lot of aggression and we were alone in the corridor. G. took the chance offered—his right fist slammed into my midriff. My sight blackened and I fell to the floor, moaning like a mademoiselle in a nineteenth-century novel. G. vanished.

As the darkness cleared I found myself staring up at a figure stooping over me. A drawn-out, whining, singing voice kept repeating as if in despair, "What's the matter? What's the matter?" I saw a pink face and very neatly trimmed chalk-white beard. The expression on the face was worried.

That voice, that face, belonged to the Latin and Greek teacher Per Venström, alias Pelle Vänster (*vänster* = left), alias Bocken. Fortunately he refrained from any kind of interrogation as to why I was lying in a heap on the floor, and he seemed satisfied when he saw I could walk away unaided. Since he showed himself to be worried and somewhat helpful, I formed the impression that Bocken was at heart a well-meaning person. Something of that impression persisted later as well, even when we had our conflicts.

Bocken's appearance was stylish, quite theatrical indeed. He usually accompanied his white beard with a dark wide-brimmed hat and a short cloak. A minimum of outdoor clothes in winter. An obvious touch of Dracula. At a distance he was superior and decorative, close up his face often conveyed a helplessness.

The half-singing intonation that characterized him was a personal elaboration of the Gotland dialect.

Bocken suffered from a chronic arthritic condition and had an emphatic limp, yet he managed to move swiftly. He always made a dramatic entrance into the classroom, throwing his briefcase onto his desk; then, after a few seconds, we knew without a doubt whether his mood was favorable or stormy. The state of the weather evidently affected his mood. On cool days his lessons could be downright jovial. When an area of low pressure hovered over us and the skies were cloudy, his lessons crawled along in a dull and fretful atmosphere punctuated by those inescapable outbursts of rage.

He belonged to the category of human being that was quite impossible to imagine in a role other than that of schoolteacher. In fact, it could be said that it was hard to envisage him as anything other than a Latin teacher.

In the course of my penultimate year at school, my own brand of modernistic poetry was in production. At the same time I was drawn to older poetry, and when our Latin lessons moved forward from the historical texts on wars, senators, and consuls to verses by Catullus and Horace, I was carried quite willingly into the poetic world presided over by Bocken.

Plodding through verses was educative. It went like this. The pupils first had to read out a stanza, from Horace perhaps:

Aequam memento rebus in arduis
servare mentem, non secus in bonis
    ab insolenti temperatam
        laetitia, morituri Delli

Bocken would cry out: "Translate!" And the pupil would oblige:

With an even temper... aah... Remember that in an even temper...
no... with equanimity... to maintain an even temper in difficult con-
ditions, and not otherwise... aah... and like in fav-... favorable con-
ditions... aah... abstain from excessive... aah... vivacious joy O
mortal Dellius...

By now the luminous Roman text had really been brought down to earth. But in the next moment, in the next stanza, Horace came back in Latin with the miraculous precision of his verse. This alternation between the trivial and decrepit on the one hand and the buoyant and sublime on the other taught me a lot. It had to do with the conditions of poetry and of life. That through form something could be raised to another level. The caterpillar feet were gone, the wings unfolded. One should never lose hope!

Alas, Bocken never realized how captivated I was by those classical stanzas. To him I was a quietly provocative schoolboy whose incomprehensible nineteen-fortyish poems appeared in the school magazine—that was in the autumn of 1948. When he saw my efforts, with their consistent avoidance of capitals and punctuation marks, he reacted with indignation. I was to be identified as part of the advancing tide of barbarism. Such a person must be utterly immune to Horace.

His image of me was further tarnished after a medieval Latin lesson dealing with life in the thirteenth century. It was an overcast day; Bocken was in pain, and his rage was just waiting to explode. Suddenly he tossed out the question: who was "Erik the Lame Lisper"? Erik had been referred to in our text. I replied that he was the founder of Grönköping.* This was

---

*The archetypal small town. According to the satirical weekly *Grönköpings Veckoblad* the town was founded by King Erik Eriksson (1216–1250), known as Erik the Lame Lisper.

a reflex action on my part stemming from my wish to lighten the oppressive atmosphere. But Bocken was angry, not simply then and there but even at the end of term when I was given a "warning." This was a brief written message home to the effect that the pupil had been negligent in the subject, in this case Latin. Since my grades for written work were all high, this "warning" presumably referred to life in general rather than to my performance in Latin.

In my last year at school our relationship improved. By the time I took my exams it was quite cordial.

Around then two Horatian stanza forms, the sapphic and the alcaic, began to find their way into my own writing. In the summer after matriculation I wrote two poems in sapphic stanzas. The one was "Ode to Thoreau," later pruned down to "Five Stanzas to Thoreau," the more juvenile parts having been erased. The other was "Storm," in the sequence "Autumnal Archipelago." But I don't know if Bocken ever acquainted himself with these. Classical meters—how did I come to use them? The idea simply turned up. For I regarded Horace as a contemporary. He was like René Char, Oskar Loerke, or Einar Malm. The idea was so naïve it became sophisticated.

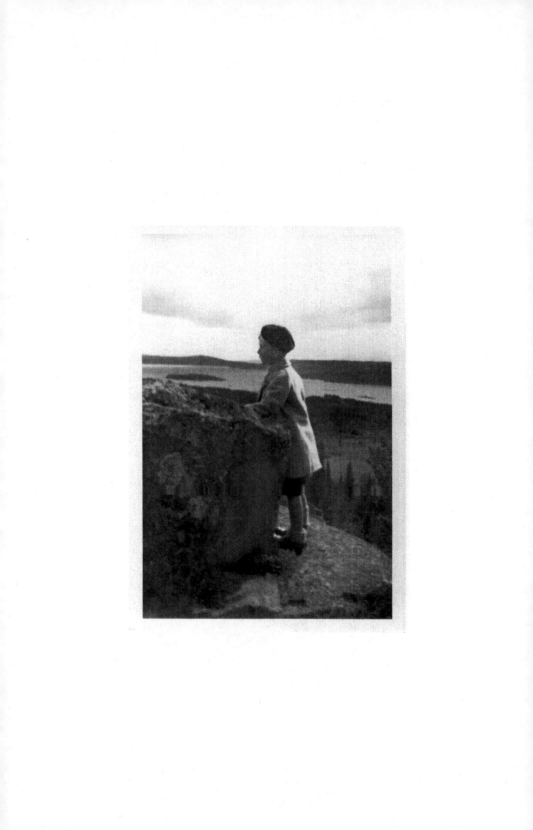

Index of titles and first lines